INDEPENDENT RADIO

Other books in the Sound Radio Series:

Radio Caroline
The story of the first British offshore radio station
by John Venmore-Rowland

Radio Onederland
The story of Radio One
by Keith Skues

INDEPENDENT RADIO

The Story of Independent Radio in the United Kingdom

by

MIKE BARON

TERENCE DALTON LIMITED
LAVENHAM   SUFFOLK
1975

Published by
TERENCE DALTON LIMITED
ISBN 0 900963 64 6

Printed in Great Britain at
THE LAVENHAM PRESS LIMITED
LAVENHAM　　　　　SUFFOLK

© Michael Baron 1975

Contents

Chapter 1	In the Beginning	9
Chapter 2	The Station of the Stars	22
Chapter 3	Just a Little Island in the Irish Sea	28
Chapter 4	The Jolly Roger Sets Sail	35
Chapter 5	An Alternative Source of Broadcasting	56
Chapter 6	A Sound Act	67
Chapter 7	The New Authority	73
Chapter 8	The Independent Local Radio Stations	87
Chapter 9	Independent Radio News	156
Chapter 10	Labour Party Halts Expansion	160
Appendix A	Addresses of the Independent Local Radio Stations and other Broadcasting Associations	167
Appendix B	For the Technically Minded	176
Appendix C	Working in Independent Radio	182
Appendix D	The Dee Jays	183
Index		189

Index of Illustrations

Broadcasting House	10
Captain L. F. Plugge	13
Reception Area	13
First radio transmitter of Radio Normandy	14
Radio Normandy vehicle	15
Reception Test Unit	16
Aerial feeder Radio Normandy	20
Aerial mast	
Radio Luxembourg team	24
Opportunity Knocks	27
Manx Radio building	29
Broadcast on Manx Radio	31
An early studio	34
Mi Amigo	36
Radio Caroline studio	36
M.V. *Galaxy*	38
Cheetah II	39
Rosko	41
Norman St John	43
Sunk Head Fort	44
Transmitter room on *Mi Amigo*	46
Radio Northsea International	48
Close-up of radio ship	50
Johnnie Walker	52
Radio Caroline	54
Paul Bryan, MP	58
Lord Annan	64
Radio Veronica	66
Christopher Chataway	69
Lord Aylestone	74
Lady Plowden	77
John Thompson	80
Janet Street-Porter and Paul Callan	88
Adrian Love	91
The radio car and traffic helicopter	97
Joan Shenton and Tommy Vance	100
Nicky Horne	106
Dave Marshall	108
A cheerful line-up	110

Adrian Juste	113
Severn Valley Railway	114
Philip Birch	114
Harry Rowell	119
Metro Radio Deejays	121
Chris Harper	123
Signing autographs	125
Bill MacDonald	127
The Three Degrees and Keith Skues	128
Gillian Reynolds	130
Radio City team	132
Ian Anderson	135
Control desk at Radio Forth	136
Plymouth Sound presenters	137
The opening of Plymouth Sound	139
Radio Trent team	142
Kid Jensen	143
Stevie Merrike	146
Dave Symonds	149
Allen MacKenzie	153
Control Room, London Broadcasting	157
Desk in newsroom of LBC/IRN	158
Graham Freer	159
Studio A at Radio Hallam	181
Deejays	186
Index	189

Acknowledgements

I would like to thank the following who either supplied information and photographs or helped in the preparation of this book:

Darryl Adams; Roger Barlow; Patricia Brigden; Donald Brooke; Terry Cassidy; Tony Churcher; George Clouston; Rodney Collins; John Guinery; David Hannon; Stephen Harris; David Heap; Phil Heap; Ian Hockridge; Peter Hulm; Tony Ingham; Dave Kindred; Sheila McCabe; Colin MacDonald; Murdoch McDonald: Geoff Moffett; Ronan O'Rahilly; Jay Oliver; Noel Osbourne; Sue Vallins.

Also the Independent Broadcasting Authority, Manx Radio, Radio Luxembourg and all the Independent Local Radio stations.

In particular my thanks to Nik Oakley, editor of the *Radio Guide,* without whose help, assistance and patience this book would not have been possible.

1 In the Beginning. . . . .

IF YOU had picked up a newspaper on the morning of Monday 8th October 1973, you would probably have noticed a news item about a new radio station: "At the ungodly hour of 6.00 a.m. today London Broadcasting launched commercial radio in Britain and smashed the BBC's 50 year old monopoly of the air." Nearly all the newspapers referred to the new radio station operated by the London Broadcasting Company as the first British Commercial Radio Station. But, in actual fact, they were very wrong. The first radio programmes with advertisements to be heard anywhere in the United Kingdom started a very long time ago.

To find out when commercial radio really began in the British Isles, we must go back to the very early days of "wireless broadcasting." Most people take radio for granted and assume it has been around for a very long time. But it was only in 1920 that the first experimental "broadcasts" were made by people like the Marconi Company of Chelmsford. In the beginning permission had to be obtained from the Post Office before a station could be set up. There were very stringent conditions over what could and could not be done. The first "broadcast" of 2LO from London was made on 11th May 1922 from a 100 watt transmitter contained in a teak cabinet and housed in a small cinema theatre on the top floor of Marconi House in the Strand. Transmissions were limited to one hour a day. Musical sounds could not be broadcast in the early programmes, as only speech was permitted. Restrictions were later relaxed and during the summer of 1922 there were regular *"live"* transmissions of concerts and musical evenings. 2LO's audience grew rapidly and by the autumn of 1922, when the BBC was formed to take over the station, it was estimated that there were nearly 50,000 'listeners-in.'

A portrait of Captain L. F. Plugge—the man who organised the first ever commercial radio broadcasts to the United Kingdom. *IBC*

Broadcasting House, home of British broadcasting for nearly half a century. *Mike Bass*

No advertisements were actually broadcast in the programmes of 2LO and the other stations, but as it was the manufacturers of wireless apparatus that operated the transmitting stations, they were a form of commercial radio. The broadcasts were intended to encourage people to purchase receiving sets made by the same manufacturers.

The Post Office had fears that a large number of transmitting stations operated by different companies would be difficult to control and would cause interference to each other. They pressed for a system which allowed only one broadcasting company.

On the 18th October 1922, the BBC was founded. The "C" didn't stand for "Corporation" but for "Company." After months of tough commercial bargaining between the wireless manufacturers and the Post Office, the British Broadcasting Company came into existence. The new company was to take over the transmitters of 2LO in London, 51T in Birmingham and 2ZY in Manchester, and be subject to Parliamentary control. Finance was to be obtained from wireless receiving licences that were being sold to the general public. This money was to be collected by the Post Office and be paid into the Exchequer.

The first broadcast of the BBC was on the 14th November and the first programmes consisted mainly of the results of the 1922 General Election that were announced on that day.

A condition of the Agreement between the Post Office and the BBC prohibited advertising. It forbade direct advertising while specifically allowing the BBC to broadcast sponsored programmes and commercial information ". . . approved for broadcasting by the Postmaster General."

Early in 1923, the BBC broadcast a concert sponsored by Harrods — the department store in Knightsbridge. In 1925, a further eight sponsored concerts were broadcast. Amongst the sponsors were the *Evening Standard,* the *News Of The World,* the *Daily Herald,* the *Weekly Dispatch, Answers* and *Titbits.* The *Daily Graphic* sponsored a concert in 1925 and again in 1926. Then the practice lapsed.

On the 31st December 1926, the British Broadcasting Company was liquidated and on the following day the British Broadcasting Corporation was constituted by Royal Charter. Transmissions were still limited only to a few hours a day and consisted of programmes of concerts, talks, religious services and short plays. There were even shows featuring jazz bands and "popular music." About one quarter of the BBC's daily transmissions in 1930 took the form of speech, but this included women's programmes, news bulletins, weather reports and the popular *Children's Hour.*

The Licence of the British Broadcasting Corporation prevented it from broadcasting advertisements. It said: "The Corporation shall not without the consent in writing of the Postmaster General receive money or any valuable consideration from any persons in respect of the sending or emitting or the refraining from sending or emitting, of any matter whatsoever by means of the stations or any of them, and shall not send or emit by means thereof any sponsored programme."

Meanwhile in Europe, radio was growing very fast, and a number of private companies were operating very powerful transmitters. Most of the Governments of European countries did not apply the severe restrictions on advertising, as Britain had done. In fact most of the stations on the continent were financed or sponsored by advertising.

As early as 1925, a commercial programme in English was directed at the UK. Radio Paris, a station which broadcast from the Eiffel Tower, presented a fashion talk in English. It was sponsored by Selfridges, but the show did not receive any advance publicity. Consequently, only three listeners wrote to the station to say they had heard the broadcast.

Two years later the radio station at Hilversum in Holland broadcast a concert intended for reception in the British Isles. It was the first of a series sponsored by Kolster Brandes Ltd. — manufacturers of radio equipment. But it was later in the 1930's that things began to happen. Captain L. F. Plugge, the man who had earlier arranged the fashion talk on Radio Paris, formed a company called the International Broadcasting Company. Radio Toulouse commenced broadcasts in English in 1929 of programmes sponsored by British gramophone companies. Two years later the International Broadcasting Company started transmissions from Radio Normandy. Programming consisted of a series of fifteen minute shows for several hours every day. By the end of 1932 there were twenty-one British firms sponsoring foreign broadcasts, including firms ". . . engaged in cigarette manufacture, food distribution, shipping, gramophone record manufacture, radio apparatus manufacture,

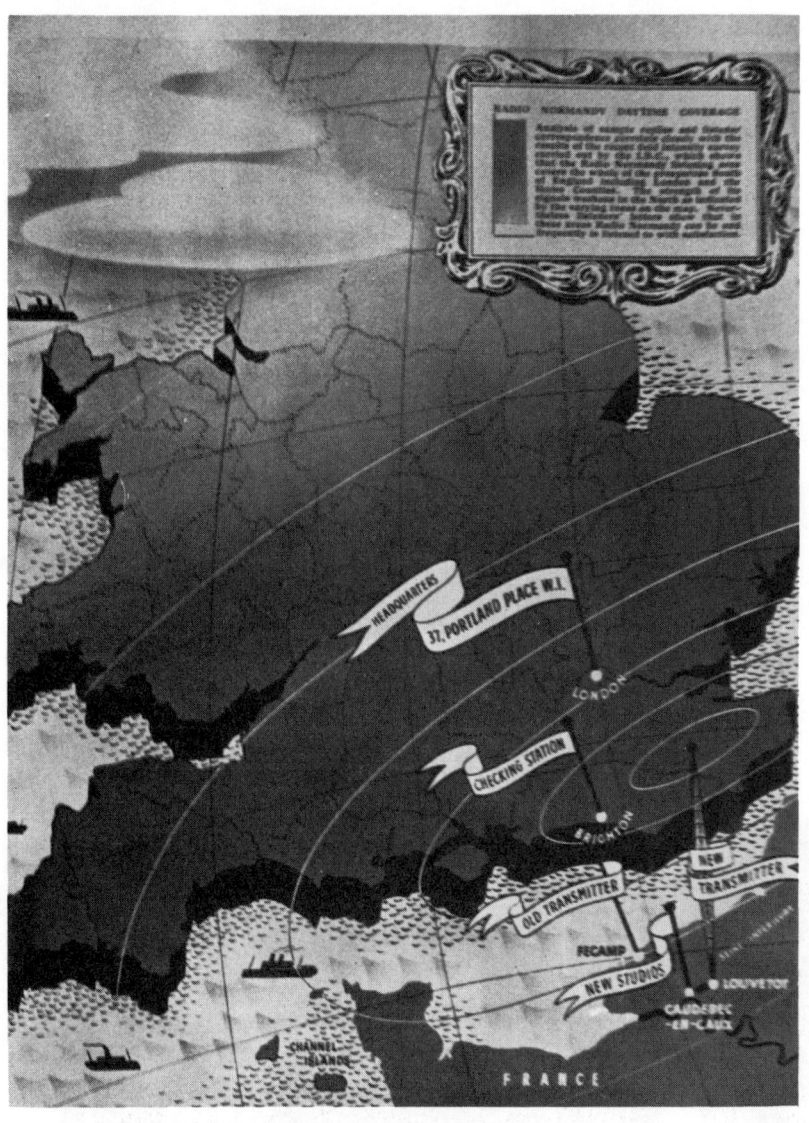

Radio Normandy's reception area.   *IBC*

the film industry, motor car distributors and retail distribution."
In 1935 British firms were spending £400,000 per year. This later
increased to £1,700,000 in 1938.

IBC experimented with broadcasts from over twenty different stations. In the mid-1930's sponsored programmes were being beamed at the UK from France, Ireland, Holland, Spain and Luxembourg. In 1936, there was a report in the press of plans for more stations broadcasting from Iceland, Eire and even from ships in International waters! But the most important stations without doubt were Radio Normandy and Radio Luxembourg. Radio Normandy was originally located in Fécamp in France. It was formerly known as Radio Fécamp, changing its name in 1929. Later a more powerful transmitter was established at Louvetot in Normandy with studios at Caudebec-en-Caux.

The International Broadcasting Company itself grew very fast. To begin with, it was just one back room and a junior typist. Later there were two back rooms, three typists, two card tables and a lot of cardboard boxes for storing audience mail. By 1939, IBC was occupying an office and studio complex in Portland Place, London. It had outside broadcast vehicles and a full-time staff of nearly 180.

The very first radio transmitter of Radio Normandy. *IBC*

The Radio Normandy outside broadcast vehicle parked outside the London headquarters of the station.   *IBC*

In 1935, IBC formed a programme production unit, with a view to providing a competent programme production service to assist the growing number of firms that were beginning to utilise radio. Between 1935 and 1939 the programme unit produced 5,000 programmes, although towards the end of the decade advertising agencies produced a substantial amount of the programming. The original studios and offices were located at 11, Hallam Street, London, W.1, but the station soon expanded to No. 9, and to 8 and 9, Duchess Street. Then by a strange irony of fate, the whole of the property was purchased by the BBC for the extension to Broadcasting House. In 1937, IBC moved *en bloc* to 37, Portland Place. The new premises covered five floors and included a total area of 100,000 square feet.

Towards the end of the thirties, IBC concentrated nearly all its efforts into Radio Normandy. The company had three outside broadcast vans, each painted black with the wording *"Radio Normandy 274 metres"* on the side. The outside broadcast vehicles made a large contribution to the programme output. They toured seaside resorts to gather material for a summer series of concert party broadcasts. The road show recorded variety artists in places as far afield as Edinburgh and Penzance. Reginald Foort was followed on his tour with the mammoth portable organ. Remote farmyards far from any electrical supply furnished radio material, and cables were laid through Gloucestershire fields to record the call of the rare marsh-warbler. IBC prided itself on "how well equipped it was in both apparatus and experience."

15

Radio Normandy was certainly a station of the stars. Many of the names of the personalities will mean nothing today, but in the thirties they meant as much as Bill Haley in the 50's, the Beatles in the 60's and the Bay City Rollers in the Seventies. The list of IBC stars included: Arthur Askey, Alice Delysia, Olive Groves, Sir Seymour Hicks, Francis Day, Reginald Foort, Clapham and Dwyer, Leonard Henry, Billy Bennett, The Two Leslies, Hutch, The Western Brothers, Tommy Trinder, Eve Becke, Les Allen, Stanelli, Donald Peers, Browning & Starr, Tessie O'Shea, Henry Tate, Leslie Jeffries, Charles Coburn, Anne Ziegler, Sam Browne, Gypsy Nina and Fred Hartley. An important part of the company's operations was the International Broadcasting Club, formed in 1932. Membership was free, and by 1939 had reached 320,000.

The other large station on the continent that beamed programmes in English at the UK was Radio Luxembourg. It didn't start until 1933 and when it did, the broadcasts on 1,191 metres long wave were from the most powerful transmitter in Europe. Programmes were initially beamed from the small Grand Duchy of Luxembourg in French, German, Luxembourgish and English. The English service began on the 4th June, 1933.

Radio Luxembourg's programmes were very similar to the IBC's shows on Radio Normandy and the other stations. In fact, in the early years of Luxembourg many of the programmes were presented by IBC. The governing body of the station was Compagnié Luxembourgeoise de Radiofusion. The transmitting station was situated in the town of Jünghstr and linked by a landline to studios in the heart of the Luxembourg City.

This Reception Test Unit belonging to Radio Normandy was frequently seen in the South East of England and the Midlands measuring the strength of the transmitted signal.

The first two sponsors of programmes were Zam Buk ("Keep a tin of Zam-Buk in the home and ready for the safe treatment of all cuts, burns and bruises") and Bile Beans ("She can slim and stay fit while she sleeps with nightly doses of Bile Beans"). The longest single running advertiser on Radio Luxembourg, the Irish Hospitals Sweepstakes, followed shortly afterwards.

One of the first announcers was Charles Maxwell. When he first worked for the station it was on a freelance basis, and he was paid at the rate of £10 per day. Later he started working full time under a contract and was paid only £10 a week!

Initially, broadcasts were only on Sundays. The programmes were recorded on sixteen inch 78 r.p.m. gramophone records in London, and shipped to Brussels, and then by train to the Grand Duchy. Every Saturday night, Charles Maxwell and another announcer, Stephen Williams, would have to go down to the station to collect the boxes of records, for broadcast the following day.

One of the most famous programmes of that era was the *Ovaltine Show* — thirty minutes of music featuring the Ovaltineys and the Ovaltineys' Orchestra.

The following is an example of the choice available to a listener in the UK on the evening of Sunday, 7th July 1935. BBC broadcasts on Sundays were limited and very sombre — there was no light entertainment at all.

Programmes in English from the Continent:

RADIO LUXEMBOURG (1304 metres longwave)

5.00 p.m.	Phillip's Live Yeast Concert. Compered by Christopher Stone.
5.30 p.m.	Entertainment Broadcast Especially For The League of Ovaltineys. Songs and stories by the Ovaltineys themselves and by Harry Hemsley.
6.00 p.m.	Take another trip with Showman Stanelli round the 3-Ring Oranges and Grapefruit World's Best Fair (Acrobats, A Performing Elephant, The Skating Rink and The Candy Store). Presented on behalf of South Africa's most delicious oranges and grapefruits.
6.15 p.m.	Spiller's "Turog" Concert.
6.30 p.m.	Rinso Concert. Davey Burnaby and his Rinsoptimists.
7.00 p.m.	Parsley Salmon Concert. With The Boys Around The Campfire.

7.15 p.m.	Monkey Brand Programme.
	Myrtle and Bertie in Bertie The House Decorator No. 5.
7.30 p.m.	David Cope Ltd., Popular Concert.
	Including a talk on the current racing by well known racing journalist, Mr Geoffrey Gilbey.
8.00 p.m.	Palmolive Concert.
	The Palmolives with Olive Palmer and Paul Oliver.
8.30 p.m.	Luxembourg News.
9.15 p.m.	Light Music and Songs.
9.30 p.m.	Ovaltine Time.
	Compered by Christopher Stone.
10.00 p.m.	Pond's Serenade to Beauty.
	The Programme for Lovers.
10.30 p.m.	Bile Beans Broadcast.
	Latest Dance Music.
11.00 p.m.	Light Orchestral Concert.
11.30 p.m.	The Past, The Present and The Future.
11.45 p.m.	Lullaby Time.
12 midnight	Goodnight — Melody and Closedown.

POSTE PARISIEN (The Paris Broadcasting Station) (312 metres medium wave).

5.00 p.m.	Concert of Light Music.
5.30 p.m.	Variety Concert.
6.00 p.m.	Request Programme.
6.30 p.m.	Orchestral Programme.
	Sponsored by Maclean Brand Stomach Powder.
7.00 p.m. –10.30 p.m.	*Off the air.*
10.30 p.m.	Sylvan Sweethearts.
	Popular Songs of Love and Romance.
	"For mountains of rich creamy lather use Sylvan Soap Flakes — giant size box — one shilling."
10.45 p.m.	Bile Beans Celebrity Concert.
11.15 p.m.	Strang's Racing Pools Variety Broadcast.
11.45 p.m.	Ingersoll Slumber Hour.
12 midnight	The Ingersoll Time Signal.
	IBC Goodnight Melody and Closedown.

RADIO NORMANDY (269.5 metres medium wave).

5.00 p.m.	Selections from Rimsky-Korsakov operas.
5.15 p.m.	Professor El Tanah's Concert.
	"For a free horoscope write to Professor El Tanah, Prince's Studio, Jersey, Channel Islands."
5.30 p.m.	Tea Time Variety.
6.00 p.m.	Request Programme.
6.30 p.m.	Hawaiian Guitar Music.
6.45 p.m.	SCO Popular Melodies.
	"Listen out for details of the new wonderful oven cleaner made by the SCO Manufacturing Company of London."

7.00 p.m. —9.30 p.m.	Programmes for French-speaking listeners.
9.30 p.m.	Military Band Concert.
10.00 p.m.	Radio Pictorial Celebrity Concert. *"Interesting articles, unusual pictures, amusing gossip — all in the Radio Pictorial every week, price 3d."*
10.30 p.m.	Light Music.
11.00 p.m.	Some Famous Symphony Orchestras.
11.30 p.m.	Popular Melodies.
12 midnight	Club Concert for Chelmsford Listeners.
1.00 a.m.	Dance Music.
2.00 a.m.	IBC Goodnight Melody and Closedown.

RADIO COTE D'AZUR (240 metres medium wave).

10.30 p.m.	Light Music.
11.00 p.m.	Celebrity Concert.
11.30 p.m.	Orchestral Gems.
12 midnight	Dance music.
1.00 a.m.	IBC Goodnight Melody and Closedown.

Such was the popularity of the continental broadcasters, that a weekly programme journal was published from 1933 to 1939. The paper, called *Radio Pictorial,* was initially 2d, (later 3d.) and was sub-titled "the all-family radio paper." Detailed programme listings for each of the stations were given, including details of the gramophone records to be played. A survey by the Joint Committee of the Incorporated Society of British Advertisers and Institute of Incorporated Practitioners in Advertising, in 1938 showed that listening levels for the foreign stations were at their highest on Sundays. For some stations the audience figures were running into millions. The survey results also showed that the total amount of listening to the foreign stations was equal in figures to that of the BBC's broadcasts.

Most of the foreign stations broadcast only on Sundays when the BBC provided only a limited service, but generally the "foreigners" proved to be more popular than the rather staid and unimaginative BBC.

Naturally the foreign broadcasters were regarded with disfavour by the BBC and the Post Office. Efforts were made to stop these stations — firstly at an international level. When Radio Luxembourg began broadcasts on longwave, it was on a wavelength not allocated to it under the Prague Plan of 1929. The Post Office made representations to the International Telecommunications Union, complaining of the use of the unauthorised frequency by Radio Luxembourg. This had little effect as Luxembourg simply ignored

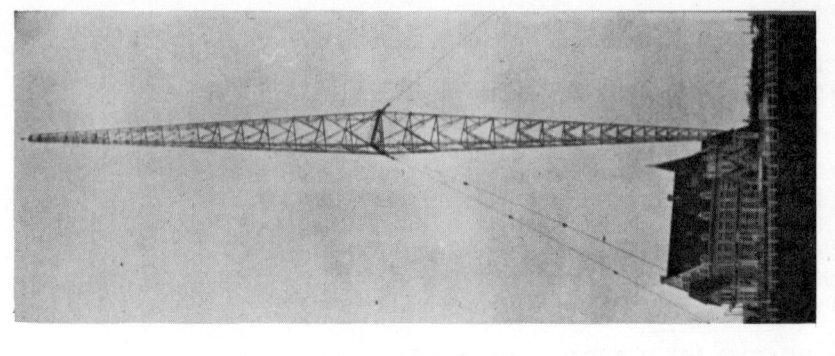

Left. The aerial feeder to the Radio Normandy aerial was suspended from a series of posts. *Right.* The transmitter building and the aerial mast. The transmitter had to be housed in a building that conformed with local architecture.

IBC

the ITU. Radio Normandy, however, was broadcasting on its authorised channel — 212 metres.

The Post Office approached the Governments of France and Luxembourg asking them to prohibit commercial broadcasts of this nature. But this was to no avail. The Post Office was also unsuccessful in attempts to pass resolutions at International Conferences on Broadcasting, which would have made the unwelcome broadcasts to the UK unlawful.

The only way the Post Office could hinder broadcasts was to refuse telephone facilities for the relaying of programmes from Great Britain to the transmitters on the continent. This it did. In consequence, many of the programmes were recorded on gramophone discs and taken to the continent for broadcasting.

But it was Adolf Hitler that closed the stations in the end. At the outbreak of the Second World War all the stations were forced to close down, and in many cases the transmitters were destroyed by the Nazis. Only Radio Luxembourg was spared. Occupied by the Germans, it was Hitler's biggest gun in his propaganda war against Britain. The infamous broadcasts of William Joyce, otherwise known as Lord Haw-Haw, were broadcast on the most powerful transmitters in Europe.

None of the stations operated by the International Broadcasting Company continued after the end of the Second World War. However, the Company did not fold. Since then it has operated a recording studio, known as IBC Sound Recording Studios Ltd., mainly producing commercials. It now holds a 13.3% share of London's all-news independent local radio station, LBC.

2 The Station of the Stars

BECAUSE of a lack of cash availability immediately after the War, Radio Luxembourg was the only station to resume broadcasts, which at first were for a limited number of hours. The English programmes moved to the present wavelength of the station, 208 metres medium wave. During the day programmes were broadcast in German and in the evenings in English, from the transmitter located in Marnach village, high in the Ardennes mountains to the north of the Grand Duchy.

Although Radio Luxembourg was back on the air, commercial support was slow in coming. Several new programme innovations came into effect at this time, including the *Top 20,* probably the longest running programme in European radio history. Teddy Johnson was the first presenter of the *Top 20* show in 1948. The original chart programme was based on the top selling sheet music and not record sales. It was compiled weekly for the Music Publishers Association. The programme attracted millions of listeners.

Many of the other programmes attracted large audiences, particularly request shows. Teddy Johnson was averaging 1,500 letters a week in 1950.

The format of sponsored programmes remained, and each show was totally financed by an individual record label, radio manufacturer or shampoo company. About 80 per cent of the programmes were recorded in the London studios, and included *Opportunity Knocks* with Hughie Green. This highly successful ITV programme started on Luxembourg. Another programme which later found its way to television, was Michael Miles' *Take Your Pick.*

Announcers and deejays who presented the sponsored programmes included names like David Jacobs, Jimmy Saville, Sam Costa, Jimmy Young and Pete Murray. Pete Murray originally went to Luxembourg for three months, but stayed for five years. As a "link man" between programmes, he earned £12. a week. He also presented a number of "live" programmes like *Monday Requests, Luxembourg's Top 20* and *Swinging U.S.A.*

Another announcer on the station at the time was Geoffrey Everett. He later became General Manager of Radio Luxembourg in London, a position he held until 1970.

It was at the beginning of the 1950's that the revenue started getting better and the station became a viable proposition. Several artists made live broadcasts from Radio Luxembourg during the 50's and 60's — names like Jackie Trent, Cliff Richard, Billy Fury, Marty Wilde and the Ted Heath Band.

Now firmly established as a record-playing station, Luxembourg had its disc jockeys. Keith Fordyce replaced Pete Murray in 1955. Don Moss, Barry Aldis and Alan Freeman (making his début on this side of the world) then joined. Later the list included Jack Jackson, Ray Orchard and Tony Brandon. In the mid 60's Tommy Vance, Don Wardell, Johnny Moran, Colin Nichol, Noel Edmonds, Stuart Grundy, Chris Denning and Barry Aldis worked from the Grand Duchy.

After the war, the BBC introduced the Light Programme. It was broadly based on the popular Forces' Service, that the BBC had operated during the war. The Forces' Service was very similar to the pre-war commercial broadcasts but without the advertising. The Light Programme was not really competition for Radio Luxembourg as the two stations catered for different needs. Luxembourg's position was only threatened with the advent of pirate radio. We shall see how the pirates caused the BBC to re-think its programming structure, and eventually introduce the pop station, Radio One.

In October 1967, within a couple of months of the pirates closing down, and shortly after BBC Radio One began broadcasting, Luxembourg changed its format. It dropped the pre-recorded sponsored shows, and introduced "personality radio." The first deejays included Paul Burnett and Tony Prince, both ex-pirates, who presented an "all-live" format. One of the first things that the new image Luxembourg did, was to discover the Osmonds, and later help break in a new artist, Alvin Stardust.

Today, a team of six deejays broadcast from studios at the Villa Louvigny, the headquarters of Radio Tele-Luxembourg (RTL).

The Radio Luxembourg team of the early 1970s. From left to right—Dave Christian, Mark Wesley, Kid Jensen, Paul Burnett and Bob Stewart.

There are also studios in the same building for RTL's other radio and television services. RTL, the parent company, is owned by the Luxembourg Government and it provides the largest single source of revenue for the Grand Duchy of Luxembourg. In second place is its thriving steel industry.

Audience research shows that every week twelve million listeners in the UK tune in to the sound of the 1,200,000 watt transmitter in Marnach, some two miles from the German border. The music format is now pure pop aimed at an under thirty-four years of age listener. Luxembourg of the 1970's acclaims itself as Britain's only national commercial radio station.

In September 1974, the station presented a special two-hour programme, sponsored by Peter Stuyvesant Cigarettes, to celebrate its fortieth anniversary. The programme traced the station's history and included recordings of Lord Haw-Haw made during the war, but never broadcast. Bob Danvers-Walker, a pioneer of commercial radio in the 1930's, was interviewed in the programme. He worked with Radio Luxembourg and Radio Normandy, and explained how commercial radio had grown to an empire before the war temporarily destroyed it in 1939. He said:

"It's so good to look over one's shoulder at the early days of commercial radio. I don't think there's really time on the air these days — and I'm so pleased that Radio Luxembourg has made time for this programme. I think it says a lot for that station.

But then the station itself is an historic building. It does stem from the very earliest beginnings and has carried on right up to the present day, whereas the new stations that are opening up haven't got any history to look back on, so that the people who are in it haven't got any history themselves."

* * *

There have only been a few other attempts since the war to broadcast programmes to the UK from the Continent. The main problem has been because of unsatisfactory reception conditions. The medium waveband is a lot more crowded now compared with the 1930's, and high audience figures are demanded by would-be advertisers.

In 1968, an attempt was made by a group of "Free Radio" supporters to beam a programme from the tiny country of Andorra located high in the Pyrenees between France and Spain. The plan was to broadcast pop music programmes hosted by deejays from the pirate stations that had recently been scuttled. Transmissions were made between midnight and 4 a.m. on 428 metres using a 400,000 watt transmitter (twice the power of Radio Luxembourg at that time). But unfortunately reception was not satisfactory in the UK, so the experiment failed after only one broadcast.

Two years later, another attempt was made using the transmitters of Radio Monte Carlo. A small group of people got together to hire the transmitters for three hours after midnight, every Saturday. The name of the station was Radio Geronimo. Radio Geronimo set out with high ideals, and plans for programmes of progressive rock. A spokesman for the station said the format would be basically rock and roll, but would extend to classical music. There were to be no station jingles, and the commercials would be more like messages from the station to the listeners. Reception in Southern England to the initial broadcasts on 205 metres was reported to be very good. After only a few months of once-a-week transmissions,

Radio Geronimo claimed an audience of 2½ million. In May 1970. it announced that it had decided not to accept any outside advertising. Sales Director Tony Secunda said in a statement: "We have done this because every advertising agency we spoke to wanted to alter our programmes to suit their advertisements and wanted to use jingles. As an alternative, Geronimo is to start its own mail-order catalogue starting with LP offers."

The station continued to broadcast for just three hours a week on Saturdays, but frequently announced plans to increase its transmissions to four hours every night of the week. It even had plans for stereo VHF broadcasts to the UK from a 300,000 watt transmitter in France, but nothing was ever heard. Radio Geronimo broadcast on 205 metres, an adjacent channel to the BBC's Radio Four transmitter on 206 metres in Folkestone on the South Coast.

During the summer of 1970, Radio Geronimo claimed that the BBC was using the Folkestone transmitter to interfere with their signal. It alleged that the BBC was putting out test tones after midnight with the intention of jamming Radio Geronimo. Naturally the BBC denied the suggestion. However, Geronimo retaliated by "jamming" the BBC. In front of a group of press photographers, the station's two deejays, Hugh Nolan and Terry Yason, threw strawberry jam all over the main entrance to Broadcasting House in London! Radio Geronimo, however, only had a short life. Towards the end of October, tapes were sent from the London studio to Monte Carlo for transmission at the weekend. But they were never broadcast. The French authorities stopped the broadcasts because the station had got behind with its payments for the transmitter hire. The station never broadcast a farewell programme.

A few months later Radio Monte Carlo commenced its own broadcasts on the same transmitter in English after midnight on Fridays, Saturdays and Sundays. Each evening it featured recorded programmes and a new callsign "Monte Carlo International." Two ex-BBC deejays Tommy Vance and Dave Cash presented the shows. Later they were joined by BBC rebel jock, Kenny Everett. The station obtained finance from commercial advertising and "plug" records — discs sponsored by record companies. The music format of Monte Carlo International was "anything progressive," although nearly all the programmes were open-ended and would stray into other music fields. Programmes were recorded in a recording studio in Fulham and flown out to Monte Carlo each week. However, during the Midem Festival at Cannes, both Tommy Vance and Dave Cash presented live programmes from a special studio.

After a couple of months, broadcasting hours were extended and Monte Carlo International beamed programmes to the UK after midnight, seven days a week. But unfortunately the odds were against it. Because of the location of the transmitters, reception in Great Britain was inconsistent and the station had some difficulty in obtaining advertising revenue. After three months, the Monte Carlo company decided there was not enough money coming in to make it worth while continuing the broadcasts. Instead they hired the transmitters out to various religious broadcasters.

Hughie Green's highly successful Thames Television programme *Opportunity Knocks* first started on Radio Luxembourg. *Thames Television*

3   Just a Little Island in the Irish Sea

AT THE end of the 1950's commercial radio broadcasts from within the UK were still a long way off, as successive Governments had deferred proposals for commercial radio stations. However, that was not the case on the tiny Isle of Man. The Island covers an area of 227 square miles and is located in the Irish Sea thirty miles from both England and Northern Ireland. Amongst other things, it boasts its own Parliament — one of the oldest in the world, the TT races and cats without tails. It has a status of partial independence and can pass its own domestic laws.

In 1959 the Manx Parliament (Tynwald) passed a Bill authorising the installation of a 100 kW medium wave transmitter on the Island. The main purpose of the station was to expand the Isle of Man tourist trade, on which the economy of the island depends, and to earn additional revenue by selling advertising to British manufacturers, who would, from such a station, be able to reach the majority of listeners in Great Britain.

However, the Manx Government had adopted the 1949 Wireless Telegraphy Act, so no broadcasting station could be operated on the Isle of Man without a licence issued by the General Post Office. The Home Office made it clear to the Manx Government that no licence for a high power radio station would be granted. It agreed that the Island could have a licence for its own radio station, provided the signal could not be heard regularly on the mainland.

The idea of a purely local radio station covering such a small population as the Isle of Man's 50,000 inhabitants did not seem a commercially viable proposition. For a considerable time no further action was taken, as the potential return was of little attraction in relation to the risks involved. However, in 1964 Richard L. Meyer and Pye Ltd. agreed to undertake jointly the formation of a company to operate a purely local station, within the limits imposed by the Home Office. Richard Meyer had been involved in commercial broadcasting for some time. From 1932 to 1940 he was General Manager of the International Broadcasting Company, responsible for developing commercial programmes from Continental Stations like Luxembourg and Normandy. After the war he was involved in commercial radio in Lourenco Marques, and later in Independent Television in the UK. When the Isle of Man Broadcasting Company Ltd. was formed, he became the Chairman. In November 1964 Tynwald unanimously approved the appointment of the company as its sole concessionaire for the operation of Manx Radio, and an agreement was signed with the company to this effect.

The Post Office had issued a licence in May of that year for experimental broadcasts on VHF. Manx Radio commenced transmissions from a studio housed in a caravan on a temporary site at Orchan near Douglas, the first programme being a commentary on the TT races on 5th June 1964. From this site the transmissions covered barely one half of the population of the island, and of those, only about 10 per cent could hear the programmes in the VHF band as some 90 per cent of set owners did not have VHF sets. That gave a potential audience of only 2,500! The station continued its experimental transmissions in the VHF band, broad-

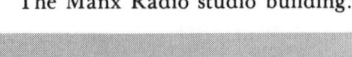

The Manx Radio studio building.

casting musical programmes for four hours a day until in October 1964 when another licence was received from the Post Office allowing Manx Radio to transmit in the medium wave band on 188 metres. The times of broadcasting were increased at intervals until, by April 1965, the station was broadcasting for ten hours a day. At the end of May, a ruling of the Performing Rights Tribunal permitted a greater use of copyright gramophone records in the programmes and transmissions were increased to twelve hours a day.

Early in 1965 a permanent site was acquired for the VHF transmitter at Foxdale, roughly in the centre of the Island. Fifteen months after the first broadcasts had been made, a further GPO licence was received permitting the station to utilise the wave length of 232 metres during daylight hours. Medium wave broadcasts were transmitted on this wavelength during the day and on 188 metres at night. These changes substantially improved reception in most parts of the Island, but did not give satisfactory coverage in the north. This had to await the erection of directional aerials. but owing to particularly bad weather during the winter of 1965-66, the completion of this work was deferred to the spring. When the directional aerials came into operation in April, satisfactory reception was at last available over the entire Island. The following month the studio in the caravan was replaced by specially built studios on the Promenade at Douglas. The Company's offices are now situated in the same building. In 1968, Pye Ltd. and Richard Meyer wanted to sell their interests in the station. The Manx Government bought all the shares, and the station is now run by the Isle of Man Broadcasting Commission, but outwardly it appears exactly the same.

During the 1960's the debate on commercial radio began to gather momentum. As Manx Radio was the only station operating, it was considered as a prototype for local commercial radio in the UK. A considerable amount of valuable information was obtained through the experience of Manx Radio. In the beginning the station had a regular staff of 14 people, two of whom were part-time. The General Manager also acted as Chief Announcer. The four full-time announcers also took on various other duties.

Operation expenditure in 1966 was estimated at between £25,000 and £26,000 per annum — almost half that amount accounted for by salaries. Programme expenses amounted to about

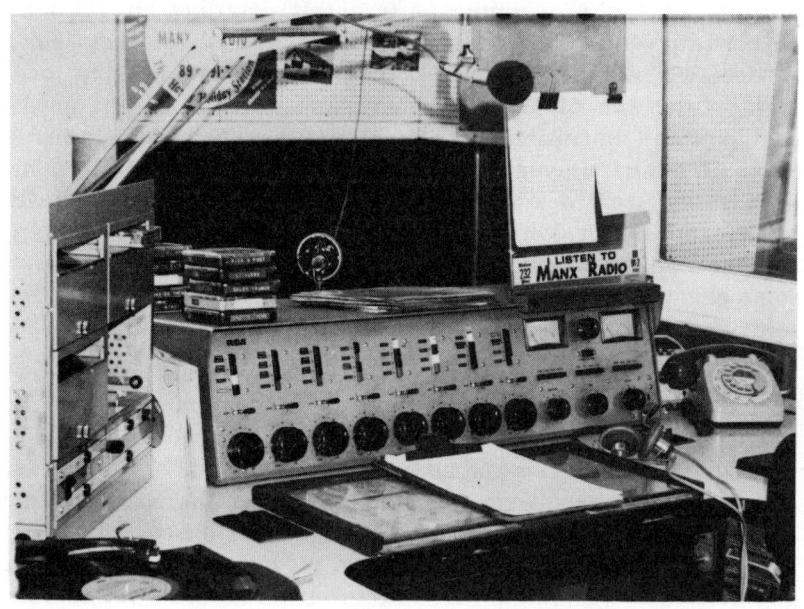

A programme being broadcast on Manx Radio.

10 per cent and included payments in respect of copyright fees to artists and record companies. Manx Radio's only source of revenue was derived from advertising. In August 1966, Richard Meyer said in a statement:

"At the present time annual expenditure is still higher than revenue, but in the twelve months ended March 31st 1966, the total orders booked exceeded the costs of operation ... Since the station only started to sell advertising in October 1964, a break even point after only two years' operation in the particular circumstances applying to Manx Radio is quite as good as could have been expected and better than many people anticipated."

The financial position of the station now appears to be very much the same, although no figures are available. Advertising rates for the station are remarkably low. A 30 second commercial at "peak" time is only £1.50.

The most important ingredient in the station's programming formula is music. Speech programmes are kept to a minimum. The purpose of the programme pattern was described in 1966 by Richard Meyer as providing the public of the Isle of Man with a service . . . "which, above all, keeps them informed of all happenings on the Isle of Man and increases awareness of the needs, problems and amenities of the community." The music output of Manx Radio has stayed much the same over the years. It doesn't broadcast a great deal of pop music but it does transmit mostly bright and better known works including film music, musical comedies and even the lighter classics. During the tourist season some changes are made in the musical content to provide for the somewhat different tastes of the holiday makers.

During the early days before Manx Radio started, there were several confrontations between Tynwald and Westminster over the island's right to have a radio station. When the Home Office finally gave in to the demands and allowed the establishment of a station on the Island, there were further battles over the power of the transmitters, The Home Office stuck rigidly to the condition that the station should not be receivable on the mainland. The station's ambition to have a more powerful transmitter broadcasting to both Britain and Europe grew stronger and this was to lead to a bitter feud between Tynwald and the British Government in 1967.

In July of that year, the British Postmaster General rejected a plea by the Manx Broadcasting Commission for an increase in power. At about the same time the Government's anti-pirate radio legislation, the Marine etc. Broadcasting (Offences) Bill was debated in the Manx House of Keys. The Bill was defeated by 19 votes to three. It appeared that the pirate station Radio Caroline North, anchored 3½ miles off Ramsey, had been given a guarantee to continue broadcasting. Many Manxmen regarded Caroline as an asset to the Island as it considerably helped in bringing tourist trade to the Isle of Man.

Any chance of the Island meekly accepting the Government action against the pirate ship had been shattered when the application for an increase in power had been refused. It had been hinted that if a more powerful Manx Radio had been allowed, the Island would have had no qualms about passing the legislation against the pirates.

At the beginning of August, the British Government stated that it would extend the Act to the Island by an Order in Council signed by the Queen. The issue developed into a wider one. The

British Government was attempting to enforce its own domestic policies on the Island against the Government's wishes.

The Island is proud of its independence. Its income tax is half the rate of the mainland and there are no stamp duties. It would have a lot to lose if the men from Westminster started meddling in its internal affairs. The anti-pirate Act was regarded by many Manxmen as only the "thin edge of the wedge." There was talk of the issuing of Manx passports, the creation of a Manx Army and a take-over of the GPO on the Island by the Manx Government.

The Order in Council came into effect on 1st September, when the Marine etc. Broadcasting (Offences) Act was extended to the Isle of Man. At first there were protests, but these quickly died away. The Island had come very close to declaring itself fully independent because of the issue. The situation would probably have never arisen if Manx Radio had been allowed the increase in its power, for which it had applied only a few months previously. At the beginning of 1974, the Manx Government instituted a Committee of Enquiry to look into the future of broadcasting on the Island. The results of the findings have not been disclosed yet, but it is possible Tynwald may ask for an increase in power again.

One report prepared by the Manx Association of Scientists, Artists and Writers (MASAW) was presented to the Government at the end of 1974. The MASAW report proposes that a two service station be developed — one station, Manx Radio, serving the Island, and a new station, Radio Irish Sea, which would be fully committed to the tourist industry. MASAW points out that there has been a considerable increase in Irish Sea traffic in recent years, owing to fruitful herring harvests and the likely development of Celtic Sea Oil. The proposal is that Radio Irish Sea provides an entertaining and informative service for the many people using the Irish Sea at one time or another. Such a service could be approved as an acceptable and appropriate function of Manx Radio and this would provide a useful argument for some additional increase in broadcasting power. During the summer months it would concentrate more on the tourist market. The report by MASAW says the station is capable of running two services and that such a system would be economically viable.

Whatever happens, it is likely that Manx Radio will be applying for an increase in power again some time in the future. Because of a growing sense of independence on the Island, Tynwald may well be able to persuade the Home Office to allow it next time. It seems to have been forgotten that Manx Radio was once the only local commercial radio station in the UK. Now it is just a small and inconspicuous part of the fast growing British radio scene. But while there is still a possibility that it may be able to increase the range of its radio transmitters and then be able to provide formidable competition for the mainland radio stations, it should never be ignored.

One of Manx Radio's early studios.

4 The Jolly Roger Sets Sail

ON EASTER Sunday, 29th March 1964, something happened that was to start a whole series of events that were eventually completely to change the whole pattern of sound broadcasting in the United Kingdom. At exactly mid-day on that date a new radio station was officially launched. Listeners tuning-in would have heard the voice of disc jockey, Simon Dee, announce:

"Hello, everybody. This is Radio Caroline on 199, your all-day music station."

The new radio station was broadcasting popular music programmes from a ship called the *Caroline,* anchored five miles off Harwich, Essex, and in International waters. She was the first of many pirate stations to appear around the coasts of the British Isles, within the next three years.

But Radio Caroline was not the first radio station to broadcast from a ship. Before Caroline arrived on the scene, there had been at least eleven commercial radio stations broadcasting from the High Seas, to various Scandinavian and Northern European countries. In fact it is believed that the first offshore radio broadcasts were made as early as the late 1930's by ships outside territorial waters, off California. A number of large ships were used to provide non-stop gambling facilities at anchorages beyond the American limits. Commercial radio broadcasts were made from some of these gambling ships for a short time.

The first real pirate in Europe was Radio Mercur, located off Copenhagen, Denmark. Transmissions began in July, 1958, from a small 107-ton German fishing boat called *The Cheeta.* Radio Mercur broadcast, on VHF, programmes of popular and light music for four years, until it was closed by armed Danish police on the 16th August, 1962.

The radio ship *Mi Amigo*.   *Dave Kindred*

Tony Blackburn in the Radio Caroline studio.   *Dave Kindred*

Several other stations had appeared off Holland, Sweden and Belgium, but most had been closed down by their respective Governments by the time Caroline arrived. Only two were still broadcasting, Radio Syd, off the Baltic coast of Sweden, and Radio Veronica, off Scheveningen, in the Hague, Holland.

The man behind Radio Caroline was a 22-year old Irish businessman, Ronan O'Rahilly. He had been involved in the music and club business and it was around 1962 that he started handling a new and unknown pop singer called Georgie Fame. He took a recording of Georgie Fame around the record companies and found that an almost monopoly situation existed. There were only the two large record manufacturers, EMI and Decca, and two smaller concerns, Pye and Phillips. The four companies, between them, accounted for 99 per cent of all record sales. All four rejected the tapes of Georgie Fame, some saying that it was too early for coloured singers in Britain. That amused O'Rahilly, as Fame was a Lancashire lad.

O'Rahilly's next step was to form his own record company, and still not fully aware of the monopoly situation, took an acetate recording to the studios of Radio Luxembourg to ask for some airplay. There, he was shocked to learn that virtually the entire Luxembourg airtime was made up by sponsored programmes, from the four big record companies. It was just not possible for Luxembourg to play anything on another label.

He then went to the BBC, where he was told that they only played established artists on their one programme a week of popular music.

"I remember thinking at that time," O'Rahilly later explained, "because my mind just worked logically, if they are not going to give me airtime, obviously the next step is to start a radio station. I didn't think about it for six or seven weeks, I just said there and then, that's what I've got to do!"

O'Rahilly was determined to smash both the monopoly of the record industry and of the sound broadcasting media. At a party a few weeks later, he was talking to some people, when a girl mentioned a pirate station called Radio Veronica operating off the Dutch coast. He saw immediately how a similar station could broadcast off the English coast.

The Radio London ship, the M.V. *Galaxy*. Dave Kindred

Immediately he set about raising finance for his project and with the aid of Irish, British and Swiss interests, obtained a 763-ton former passenger ferry, the *Frederica*. The ship was moved to Greenore, a port in the Irish republic owned by Ronan's father, Aodhagan O'Rahilly. Here the ship was fitted out with the radio equipment, including a 165ft. high aerial mast and a special anchor. All the work was done with a considerable amount of secrecy.

The ship left Greenore fully equipped and with a new name, *Caroline*, on the 26th March. Under the command of Captain Baeker, she sailed in International waters around the coast, eventually dropping anchor on the following day, Good Friday. The ship was located in a position four miles off Felixstowe, just outside territorial waters and safely clear of the main shipping lanes. Test transmissions commenced the same day, and two days later the first official programme was broadcast. The first disc in the programme presented by DJ Chris Moore was the Beatles with *Can't Buy Me Love*. Britain's first pirate commercial station was on the air.

The *Evening Standard* on the 9th April reported that Radio Caroline had received more than 20,000 fan letters in its first ten days of broadcasting. But it was not until May Day 1964, that the first advertisement was transmitted. It was for the Duke of Bedford's Woburn Abbey. Later he reported that instead of four thousand people, some 4,500 had turned up the next day in spite of the fact that it was very wet.

But O'Rahilly had not been the only man thinking of running his own radio ship. A forty-two year old Australian, Mr Allan Crawford and his company, Project Atlanta, had been planning an offshore station since 1962. But a number of the backers of the station pulled out when the Danish pirate, Radio Mercur, was seized by the police.

Radio Nord had been a Swedish pirate station, operating from the M.V. *Bon Jour*. It was forced to close down when the Swedish Parliament passed a bill outlawing offshore radio, which took effect from the 1st August, 1962. Crawford had negotiated with the station, shortly before its closure, to purchase the radio ship complete. A price and delivery date were agreed and after Radio Nord's final broadcast, the *Bon Jour* went to El Perol in Spain to be overhauled. Then, in a renovated condition, she was delivered to a position at the mouth of the Thames. It may even have broadcast then as around that time there were reports of a mysterious "Radio LN" testing on 306 metres.

But then Crawford's financial backers would not fulfil their obligations, and Crawford was short of money. The American and Swedish owners were not prepared to offer credit facilities, so the *Bon Jour* was moved to Ostende, and then Houston, Texas, where it was to be converted into a luxury yacht for its American owners.

Eventually, Project Atlanta found new investors, and £55,000

The *Cheetah II*, a temporary home for Radio Caroline after its own ship ran aground in 1966. *Dave Kindred*

was raised to buy the radio ship and bring it back to Europe. The vessel, now re-named the M.V. *Mi Amigo,* was taken to Greenore — the same port as Radio Caroline was using — for the fitting of a new transmitting mast. But because of the race between the two radio ships to be first on the air, and the fact that O'Rahilly's father owned the port, all work on the *Mi Amigo* had to be done just outside in the bay.

The M.V. *Mi Amigo* did not leave Greenore until the middle of April, then after a few days at sea, dropped anchor three and a half miles east of Frinton-on-Sea, Essex, within sight of Radio Caroline. Regular programmes started on the 12th May 1964, on a wavelength of 201 metres, very close to Caroline on 199 metres.

Both stations fought for the same audience and advertisers, but only for a short time. On the 2nd July, a merger between the two pirates was announced. The original Caroline ship was to move to an anchorage off the Isle of Man and become Radio Caroline North. Meanwhile Radio Atlanta in the Thames Estuary would change its name to Radio Caroline South. It was estimated that the two radio ships were together attracting an audience of over six million listeners. There was no doubt that the new stations were popular. The Post Office had to arrange special deliveries of listener mail to the new offices at Caroline House, 6, Chesterfield Gardens, just off Curzon Street, and near Park Lane.

But the success of Caroline had not gone un-noticed by others, and it wasn't long before other pirates jumped on the bandwagon. Britain's third pirate set sail on 27th May. It was to be called Radio Sutch after its organiser, pop singer Screaming Lord Sutch. Sutch was a long haired and extrovert singer, who had previously gained publicity by standing in a Parliamentary by-election as a candidate for the Independent Teenage Party. As part of a publicity stunt, he equipped a 60-foot fishing trawler, the *Cornucopia* with a transmitter and headed for the High Seas. Completely by accident he discovered in the mouth of the Thames Estuary and apparently in International waters, an abandoned anti-aircraft gun tower. The tower was called Shivering Sands Fort and was one of several built during the Second World War. The structure consisted of a complex of six separate forts perched 100 feet above the sea on stilts and linked together by catwalks. The army used them during the war as gun emplacements, but they had since fallen into a derelict condition.

One of Caroline's most popular disc jockeys was Rosko, pictured here in the studio. *Dave Kindred*

Sutch loaded his equipment on to the Shivering Sands Fort and broadcasts started soon after. However the signal was very weak and only audible over a small area of the mainland. Programmes were of a very poor standard. Frequently records were not introduced, and whole sides of albums were played. Most of the discs in the station's "library" were by Sutch himself. The new pirate did not pose any serious competition to Caroline.

As soon as Sutch had landed on the fort, the War Office (as it was then known) issued a statement that the broadcasters were trespassing on Government property. But later Whitehall announced it was investigating the legal position and that it was not clear which Government department should be responsible for evicting the "squatters." As a result, no action was taken, and before long another similar set of towers was being occupied.

In July 1964, Radio Invicta, a "good-music" station began operating from Red Sands Fort, about a mile further out to sea from the Radio Sutch Fort. It was similar to Sutch, in that it lacked the professional organisation of Radio Caroline. Run by local fisherman, Tom Pepper, it only lasted a few months. On the night of 16th December, Pepper was returning to the shore with a disc jockey and an engineer, when the small supply boat sank, causing the loss of all three lives.

Two former partners of Pepper took over the station which changed its name to Radio King. Meanwhile, Lord Sutch had lost interest in his radio station, and in September his manager, Reg Calvert, took over. The station became known as Radio City.

But these were just two small pirate stations. Just before Christmas 1964, the most powerful radio ship yet to take to the air, arrived in the Thames Estuary. The 780-ton *Galaxy* had been fitted out in Miami with a 50,000 watt transmitter and 212 foot high mast, 23 feet higher than Nelson's Column. Initially, the *Galaxy* was anchored inside territorial waters, and only moved after Caroline's boss O'Rahilly warned the owners of their error. It moved up the Essex coast to a point about a mile away from the M.V. *Mi Amigo*.

On Christmas Eve, regular transmissions commenced from the new pirate, Radio London. This station, or "Big L" as it became known, was backed by American businessmen who had invested half a million pounds. Managing Director was Philip Birch, a man whose name is still linked with successful commercial radio today. Birch, who had a background with advertising agencies in the States, brought with him a slick, professional style of salesmanship and broadcasting. From the very start, "Big L" had catchy American jingles and professional disc jockeys. On a wavelength of 266 metres, close to the BBC's Light Programme, Radio London soon built up a massive following and overtook Caroline in the popularity stakes.

The pirate radio boom was now gathering momentum. Newspapers were full of plans for new stations, and many amateur stations appeared sometimes for a couple of days, or even just a couple of hours! But running a pirate station was an expensive business as many found to their cost. Many ambitious plans never got off the ground because of the high costs involved.

It wasn't until 1966 that competition between the pirates got to its fiercest level. During 1965, both Radio City and Radio King increased the power of their transmitters. Radio Essex came on the air in November from another deserted Tower in the Thames Estuary. Radio King became Radio 390 with new owners, new programming, a new frequency and increased power. Radio 390 had a very different format to Caroline, London and City — instead of playing pop music it featured "sweet and light" music, and introduced a new expression to the UK, "Middle of the Road music."

By the end of 1965, it was estimated that as many as fifteen million listeners were tuning in regularly to a pirate station. At the end of the first year of operation, Radio London announced that it had made a profit.

"Radio Scotland, swinging to you on 242" was the first sound that many listeners in Scotland heard, as the bells tolled in the New Year of 1966. And yet more pirates were to follow. But during January of that year, tragedy struck Radio Caroline. On the evening of the 19th, the *Mi Amigo* started dragging her anchor at the height

Norman St John in the Radio London studios. *Dave Kindred*

Radio Tower attempted unsuccessfully to broadcast from Sunk Head Fort for a short time. *Dave Kindred*

of a storm. The crew did not realise until too late, and the ship was grounded only fifty yards off the Frinton beach.

The following day when the tide went out, it was possible to walk completely around the crippled radio ship. Re-floating the *Mi Amigo* was a very difficult operation, and when it did eventually get back to sea, a team of divers found that damage had been done to the hull. It was necessary for the ship to go into a dry dock in Zaandam in Holland, for repairs. But Caroline was not off the air for very long. While the 470-ton *Mi Amigo* was in Holland, the Caroline Organisation hired another radio ship, the *Cheetah II* from the owner of Radio Syd, a Swedish pirate station. Pack ice in the Baltic had forced Radio Syd to stop broadcasting and move from its anchorage. Transmissions of Radio Caroline originated from the *Cheetah II* for three months, until its own boat returned, this time with a new 50,000 watt transmitter and a new wavelength, 259 metres.

For a short time, a station called Radio Tower operated from another Thames Estuary fort, called Sunk Head, fourteen miles from Walton on the Naze, Essex. There were also plans to operate

Tower Television from the same fort. Programmes were to be broadcast each evening for three hours after the BBC and ITV had closed down. It was claimed that test transmissions were made by the pirate television station, but there are no reports of anyone ever receiving them on the mainland. Neither the radio nor the television station ever became fully operational. It was found that it was impossible to supply the fort, in rough weather, so it was abandoned. A year later a team of twenty Royal Engineers landed on the fort to commence demolition. The superstructure was cut away and on 21st August 1967, 2,200 lbs. of explosives were used to blow up the tower, so as to prevent any further unwelcome squatters moving in.

Early in 1966, National Opinion Polls Ltd. carried out a number of surveys to establish the size of the audience to commercial radio. It was found that 45 per cent of the population listened to an offshore station and/or Radio Luxembourg during a week. The following figures were quoted in the results:

Radio Luxembourg	8,818,000
Radio Caroline	8,818,000
Radio London	8,140,000
Radio 390	2,633,000
Radio England	2,195,000
Britain Radio	718,000

Not only did the pirate stations have big audiences — they were making a lot of money. After eighteen months on the air, Caroline announced it had grossed over £750,000 in advertising revenue. Radio London, after only two months on the air, had obtained £200,000 worth of advertising contracts. In March of the following year, it was selling £75,000 of commercials a month. The advertising rates for both Radio Caroline and Radio London were around £120 for a one minute commercial at peak time. That was equivalent to 6d (2½ new pence) per thousand listeners — certainly an economical way of advertising.

More pirates arrived on the scene. In May 1966 a highly Americanised and ambitious operation involving two stations from one ship - Swinging Radio England and a light music station, Britain Radio — came on the air. And in June, Radio 270 which was anchored off Scarborough, began broadcasting to Yorkshire. Radio 390 announced plans of buying another pirate ship, which would be anchored off the North of England as Radio 390 North.

Radio London increased power to 75 Kilowatts and talked about a sister station it was to start, called Radio Manchester. Radio Caroline, not to be outdone, stated that the North ship's power would be increased by five times, by using a new transmitter it had acquired.

Obviously, the situation was heading towards chaos. At the rate of progress of pirate radio, it was estimated that there would have been a hundred pop pirates on the air by the end of the decade, if something wasn't done soon!

The Labour Government had been anxious not to do anything that was against public opinion, especially during the period before the General Election in 1966. The first Postmaster General to be involved in the pirate radio saga was Tory Mr John Bevin. He was first questioned in the House of Commons about Radio Caroline in February 1964, before it had even begun operating. He stated that the transmission of commercial radio programmes from ships at sea was breaking international regulations, and endangering international agreements about sharing frequencies. He went on to say that it would almost certainly cause serious interference to radio communications in Britain and other countries and hinted that legislation might be introduced to deal with it. That was the first of many threats to be issued by three Postmaster Generals.

In the Autumn of 1964 there was to be a General Election. Both Labour and Conservative MP's realised that the pirates had audiences

The transmitter room on the *Mi Amigo*.　　　　　　　　　　*Mike Bass*

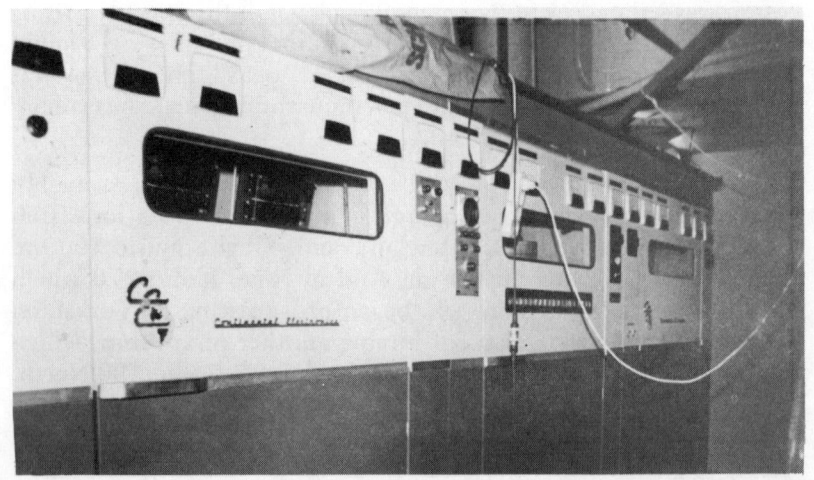

of millions. Neither Party wanted to make it an Election issue for fear of losing vital votes. As it happened, Labour won but only with a slender majority. For two years, Prime Minister Harold Wilson sat on a knife-edge, and it was decided unofficially that no unpopular action should be taken against the pirates.

At the second General Election in 1966, Harold Wilson and his party were returned with an increased majority. Now was the time to do something. Throughout most of the pirate era, the Postmaster General was Mr Anthony Wedgewood Benn. Benn was constantly questioned about the pirates in the House of Commons. Each time he promised legislation, but nothing seemed to happen. It was the events of June 1966 which hit the headlines of the nation's newspapers and which eventually forced the Government's hand. It all surrounded Radio City.

At the end of 1965, negotiations took place between Radio Caroline and Radio City. Plans of a take-over were considered, whereby Caroline South would broadcast from the Shivering Sands Tower and the *Mi Amigo* would move either to the North East of England or to the Bristol Channel.

Another takeover bid came from Radio London who wanted to run a new light music station, called UKGM (United Kingdom Good Music). Two Radio London deejays, Keith Skues and Duncan Johnson visited Shivering Sands Fort to inspect the station in June, and City's deejays visited "Big L's" offices to be told of their new jobs. UKGM was due to start in July 1966.

But things did not go according to plan. During the negotiations with Caroline a 10 Kilowatt transmitter was loaned to Radio City. It was delivered to the fort, but apparently never worked. Calvert, the owner of Radio City, had not paid for the £10,000 transmitter, and plans were made by the owners to recover it. The owners were apparently Major Oliver Smedley and Project Atlanta — the company that merged with Caroline in 1964. Caroline later claimed it had severed its connections with Project Atlanta in December 1964.

Early on Monday 20th June 1966, Major Smedley led a party of eleven Gravesend ship-riggers to the fort, arriving at 3.00 a.m. They managed to gain access and took over the station. The raiders held the deejays and kept Radio City off the air. Smedley left the fort shortly after the takeover. The following day Calvert and

47

Radio Northsea International—a pirate radio station that didn't arrive until 1970.
Dave Kindred

Smedley met in London, where Calvert threatened to remove the raiders by using nerve gas. Later in the evening he visited Smedley at his home. When the door was opened by a secretary, Calvert forced his way in. A scuffle developed and the Major appeared with a shotgun, and seeing the Radio City owner about to bring a heavy statue down on his assistant, shot him dead.

The following day Police visited Shivering Sands and questioned the raiders. A few days later on the Sunday evening the raiding party left, taking with them the transmitting crystal. Unknown to the boarding party, there was another piece of the vital transmitting equipment hidden on the fort, and within a short time Radio City was back on the air. Dorothy Calvert, the wife of the dead man, took over control of the station.

Several months later Major Smedley appeared at Chelmsford Assizes charged with manslaughter. The jury, after only a few seconds consideration, found him not guilty.

The dramatic raiding of the station and the tragedy which resulted hit the front pages of the leading newspapers. No longer could the Government pretend the pirates didn't exist. Action had to be taken.

On the 1st July Tony Benn announced that legislation to curb the pirates would be introduced before the summer recess. But a few days later in a cabinet re-shuffle, Benn became Minister of Technology. As a Postmaster General, Benn had been considered a miserable failure. The new man was former Chief Whip, Mr Edward Short. He was strongly opposed both to the continuance of pirate radio and the introduction of commercial radio. He strongly believed that broadcasting should be the responsibility of a public body. The new Postmaster General immediately set to work on an anti-pirate law, based on an agreement reached at the Council of Europe in January 1965. It would make it an offence to establish or operate such stations, or give them any form of assistance. Mr Short meant business.

The pirates reacted in style. Radio 390 invited listeners to write to their Member of Parliament. Radio Caroline issued stickers and Radio England put in a formal application for a licence. Off Scarborough, Radio 270 invited the Opposition spokesman on Broadcasting to go on board the radio ship.

On 27th July, the Marine etc., Broadcasting (Offences) Bill received its first reading in Parliament. It covered any structure fixed, floating or airborne from which broadcasts could be made. The law, however, only affected British citizens, who owned, worked for, or aided an offshore radio station. It would have no effect on, for example, Americans, Canadians or Australians. Anyone providing, installing or repairing radio equipment would be committing an offence. Anyone taking part in a broadcast or advertising goods or services, on any station directly or through an advertising agent, would be committing an offence. Any newspaper or magazine publishing programme details would also be committing an offence. The maximum penalty was £400 or three months' imprisonment, or both. The Bill was intended to be far reaching. But it took a year before it finally became law.

The pirates immediately saw the loopholes in the Bill. They could employ American deejays and Dutch crews, be tendered from Holland and rely on advertising from Continental advertisers, and still be within the law. They were also determined to fight.

Radio 270 was the first station to invite listeners to join the "fight for free radio" and continually asked them to write to their MP's.

A large number of MP's pressed for the bill to be delayed, and to come into effect only after a suitable alternative had been set up. Many proposals were put forward, including a BBC all-pop station called Radio 247, possibly with commercials. Another put forward plans for local commercial radio, while the BBC asked for Local Radio Stations financed by licence revenue, and an increase in licence fees.

A move against the pirates came as a surprise in September 1966 when Radio 390 was suddenly served with summonses alleging that the station . . . "situated 8½ miles off the coast but within the Thames Estuary, did unlawfully use apparatus for wireless telegraphy, namely a transmitter . . . contrary to Section One of the Wireless Telegraphy Act 1949."

Eight days later Mr Roy Bates of Radio Essex was served with a similar summons, alleging use of a transmitter without a licence from Knock John Fort in the Thames. The GPO had decided that the forts were within the territorial limits. Only one fort-based station, Radio City, remained unsummonsed. That fort had been the scene of the dramatic events of a year before. The police had been unable to intervene then as the structure was considered to be in International waters. But in January of the following year, Radio City was also summonsed to appear before the magistrates.

Close-up of the radio ship. *Dave Kindred*

At the court cases of the three pirates, all held separately, pleas of not guilty were entered. There then followed lengthy legal arguments over whether or not the Bench could try the case as the pirate radio operators claimed it was outside their jurisdiction. But the case was ruled in order, and each station was found guilty and fined. Appeals were lodged, but the High Court upheld that an Order in Council of September 1964 meant that the mouth of the Thames Estuary could be considered as a bay and that its base line ran from Walton-on-Naze to North Foreland. The three pirate towers were within this line. One by one, they all closed down.

Just before Christmas, a White Paper was published by the Government, detailing plans for a re-structured BBC. It was to be allowed to run a popular music service on 247 metres and also to set up nine experimental local radio stations, operating only on the VHF band.

As the Second Reading of the Marine etc., Broadcasting Offences Bill approached in February 1967, the fight by the offshore radio stations mounted in intensity. A new supporters association was formed on behalf of the listeners of the offshore stations. It was to become known as the Free Radio Association. Announcements inviting membership of the FRA were then broadcast on Radios 270, 390, Caroline and Scotland. The new Association distributed car stickers, leaflets, badges and strongly worded petition forms. But the Association had arrived too late. The Bill was given its second reading in the Commons and after a heated debate was passed 300 votes to 213, a Government majority of 87.

Meanwhile, the American-backed ventures Radio England and Britain Radio, both operating from the *Laissez Faire* had run into financial trouble. In March, the parent company, Peer Vick Ltd, went into liquidation declaring a loss of more than £100,000 in just one year's operations. A new company, Carstead Advertising Ltd, took over the ship and Britain Radio became Radio 355.

After a stormy passage through the House of Lords, the Bill returned to the Commons for a final reading on 30th June. Then it needed just the Royal Assent by the Queen. The Marine, etc., Broadcasting (Offences) Act was to come into effect on the 15th August 1967. The pirates announced plans for continuing after the Bill became law and started opening offices on the Continent. At the end there was just five pirate ships left — Radio Scotland, Radio 270, Radio London and the two Radio Caroline vessels.

Johnnie Walker, one of the disc jockeys who stayed on Caroline after the 14th August 1967, but later joined the BBC and is now one of the most popular deejays on Radio One. *BBC*

Wilf Proudfoot of Radio 270 announced that his station had never broken the law and did not intend to do so in the future. The pirate would close down a few seconds to midnight on the day before the Act became law. Radio Scotland had been losing money, so decided that it too would not evade the law, and would close down on the same day.

Only two stations seemed prepared to fight on, Radio London and Radio Caroline. But only a few weeks before the fatal day "Big L's" boss, Philip Birch, announced that Radio London would not, after all, be attempting to stay on the air. Only Caroline remained defiant. It continually stated that if there were any prosecutions against the station or any of the staff, it would appeal to the International Court of Human Rights in Strasbourg.

O'Rahilly pointed out that the new law would make Caroline internationally recognised and legal. The Irishman explained:

"If a British shopkeeper sells cigarettes to a Radio Caroline announcer, he becomes a criminal. If the Archbishop of Canterbury or Cardinal Heenan or the Chief Rabbi give a sermon, they would become criminals. If a journalist writes a newscast or talks on Radio Caroline, he becomes a criminal. If a British advertiser advertises on Radio Caroline, he too becomes a criminal.

"But on the other hand, if the Pope was to write a sermon for Radio Caroline, he would not be a criminal, nor would any foreign International figure who wanted to use the medium to voice publicly something he wanted to say. In other words, all it does is stifle the freedom of the British subject to speak where he likes about what he likes."

On 14th August 1967, the powerful Radio London broadcast its final programme and at a few minutes past 3 p.m., the transmitter was switched off for the last time. Later in the evening Radio 270 and Radio Scotland said their goodbyes. Only Caroline remained, and at midnight proudly announced that it had become Caroline International. O'Rahilly was delighted that the other pirates had given up. He now claimed that the two Caroline ships had captured the entire twenty-five million offshore radio audience, thus making it the largest commercial radio station in the world.

Two British deejays, Johnnie Walker and Robbie Dale, continued to broadcast in defiance of the Marine Offences Act. Offices were opened in Toronto, Paris, New York and Amsterdam. Advertisements continued to be broadcast, many for British companies and products and included many "dummy" advertisements intended to confuse the GPO who were monitoring the station's broadcasts.

But the era of pirate radio was over, in spite of Caroline's brave attempt to fight the Government. On 30th September 1967, the BBC's new four channel sound service came into operation. Out went the old Home Service, Light Programme and Network Three. Instead it was to radio by numbers:

Radio One — a new pop music service on 247 metres only;
Radio Two — a "revamped" Light Programme on long wave;
Radio Three — the old Third Programme; and
Radio Four — the old Home Service.

The BBC had gone overboard for ex-pirate deejays, mostly from Radio London. Well known deejays like Tony Blackburn, Dave Cash, John Peel, Keith Skues, Ed Stewart, Emperor Rosko, Stuart Henry and Duncan Johnson, all came ashore to work for the Corporation's new pop radio station. Even the *Radio One is Onederful* jingles and station identifications were similar to the

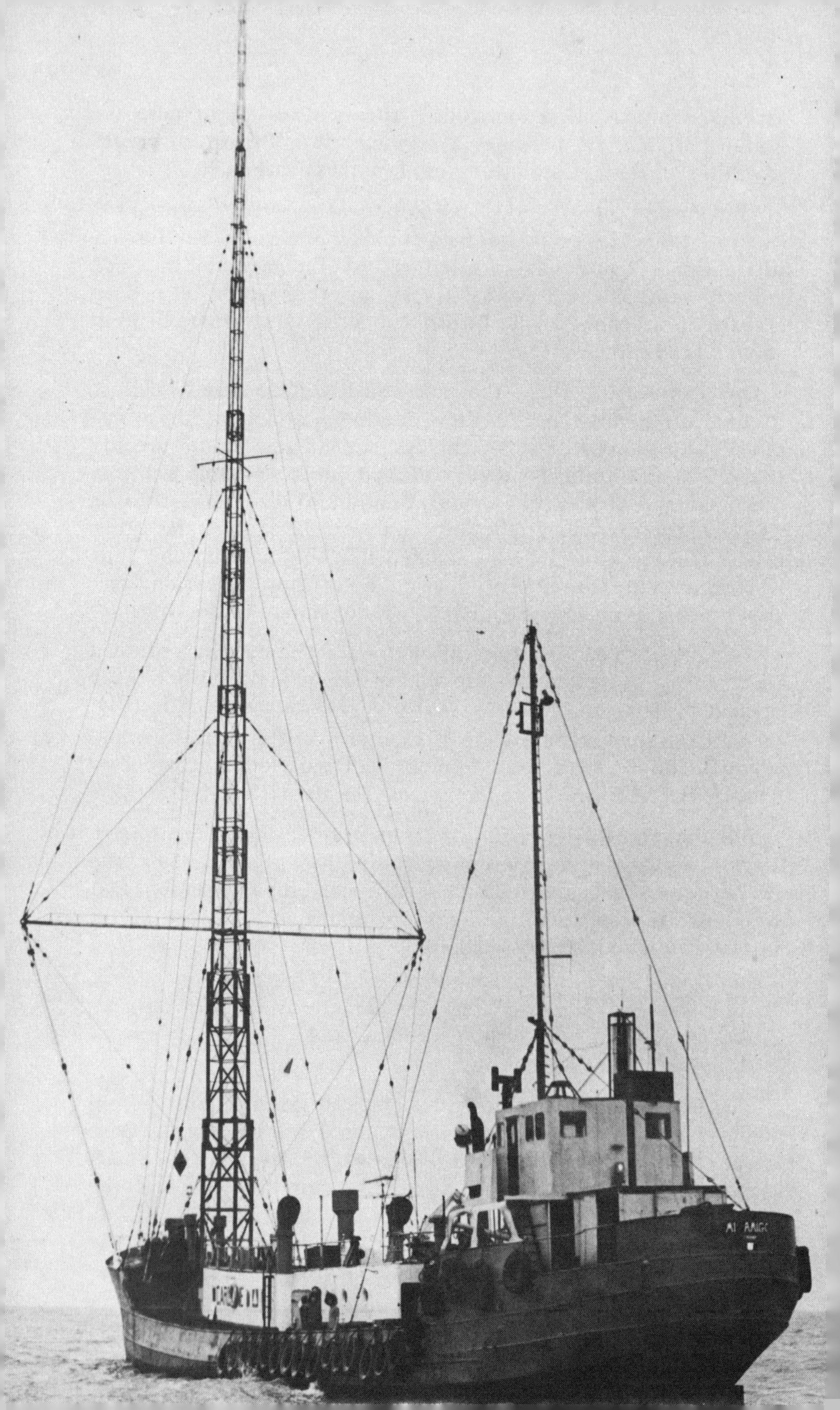

Wonderful Radio London set. Altogether it was a similar overall sound in presentation to that which the pirates had pioneered.

Most of the listeners soon forgot about the pirates, and accepted the new Radio One. But Caroline continued with a much smaller audience. It is still broadcasting today, nearly twelve years after it started (although it was off the air between 1968 and 1972). The Radio Caroline of the mid-1970's, however, is very different. Instead of relying solely on advertising revenue for its income, it hires out its powerful 50,000 watt transmitter to a Belgian business concern, called Radio Mi Amigo. They use the transmitter during the day to broadcast programmes to Europe in Dutch and Flemish. Caroline itself only broadcasts in the evenings and throughout the night. No longer is it selling baked beans and soap powder. Now it has a new message to sell — love and peace.

The most important thing about the pirate era was that it showed the people what commercial radio could sound like, and the people seemed to like what they heard. It made the BBC re-consider its ideas and attitudes towards broadcasting and introduce Radio One and Radio Two — both modelled on the pirates. In the short period that the offshore stations existed, the entire record market changed. Many new independent record companies were formed, and because of the tremendous amount of air play given to new discs, hundreds of pop groups and singers were "discovered."

The most important outcome of the pirate era as far as this book is concerned, was that there was now a considerable amount of support for the case for introduction of legal commercial radio into the UK. In 1970, it was to become an Election issue.

Radio Caroline anchored twelve miles off Frinton-on-Sea, Essex during the summer of 1975. *Dave Kindred*

5 An Alternative Source of Broadcasting

COMMERCIAL Radio has taken a long time to come to the British Isles. In other parts of the world, the whole broadcasting system has grown from local commercial radio beginnings. Radio started at about the same time, in the States, as it did in the UK. The very first American radio stations broadcast sponsored commercial programmes and in the 1930's and 1940's commercial radio spread across the USA at an incredible rate. And it is still growing today. In July, 1974, the number of commercial broadcasting stations on medium wave was 4,467 with a further 2,713 operating on the VHF band — that's approximately 150,000 American radio receivers to every radio transmitter!

But in Britain, successive Government Committees appointed to decide the future of British broadcasting, rejected the idea of commercial radio. The first, the Crawford Committee in 1926, found that there was no need for commercial radio. They preferred the idea of a public monopoly controlling the airwaves. It was turned down again in 1935 by the Ullswater Committee and in 1950 by the Beveridge Committee. The latter opposed commercial television, as well as commercial radio, but the Conservative Government did introduce independent television in 1955.

Another major enquiry into broadcasting and its future in the British Isles was set up in 1960. The Pilkington Committee reconsidered the whole sphere of radio broadcasting. It, too, rejected suggestions that the BBC's services should carry advertising, and considered that the three sound channels — the Home, the Third and the Light Programmes were adequate. There was no need for another national station — BBC or otherwise. However, it did consider the introduction of local radio, and suggested that the BBC be allowed to set up six stations immediately. Following that, further stations should be brought into operation at the rate of eighteen every year, until there were eighty broadcasting. The Pilkington Committee estimated they would be operating by March

1968, and that the total cost would be £1,400,000. Their estimate of annual running costs (for all eighty stations) was only £2,800,000, as the proposed stations would only broadcast for five hours a day!

But the Government of the day decided not to take note of Pilkington's suggestions for local radio, as they considered there was no evidence of public demand for it. Since the 1950's television had dominated any debate on commercial broadcasting. But the appearance of the pirates around the British coastline in the mid-60's revived the question of commercial radio. The question of who should control and operate broadcasting stations has always been a political issue. For the Labour Party, it has been against its principles to assign a valuable communications media to a private concern. Broadcasting is a public service and so, according to the Socialist view, should be in the hands of a public body, like other public services such as gas, electricity, water, transport, etc.

The Conservative Party, however, are advocates for private enterprise and the de-nationalisation of the public services. It maintained that a number of radio stations owned by private enterprise and competing with each other would improve standards. If there was no competition, there was no incentive for any improvement in the service already being provided. Throughout the pirate era, the Conservatives were very aware of the popularity of the offshore stations, and while in opposition, continually pressed for the introduction of commercial radio. They were, however, very worried about appearing to approve of something that was against the law. Towards the end of the decade, after all the pirates had been sunk, the leading personalities of the Party began to talk more and more about the need for an alternative source of broadcasting.

In 1970, there was another General Election and the Conservative Party announced its intention to introduce commercial radio in its manifesto. Key policymaker and Tory spokesman on broadcasting, before the Election, was Mr Paul Bryan, a director of Granada TV Rentals. In June, 1970, in an interview, he talked about the Tory plans. He proposed a network of about twenty local stations operating in obviously lucrative centres such as London, Birmingham and Manchester. During the day they would broadcast simultaneously on medium and VHF frequencies, but on VHF only at night.

The service would come under the general supervision of an independent broadcasting authority similar to the Independent Television Authority, but apparently less cumbersome. In the Conservative manifesto it said, "Local newspapers, particularly, will have a stake in local radio, which we want to see closely associated with the local community." The Newspaper Society, which represented almost all non-national newspapers, was not enthusiastic about the Tory plans, but resigned ". . . if we've got to have commercial local radio, then indeed we want to be in on it."

Labour Minister of Posts and Telecommunications, Mr John Stonehouse, was not impressed by the Conservative proposals. He had been responsible for overseeing a BBC experiment of eight local stations, which he considered to be a success. "I believe the BBC are doing an excellent job providing a wide variety of programmes," said Stonehouse in February. "No country in the world has a better sound broadcasting service. The Government don't want commercial local radio to happen in Britain. That is why we have decided that local broadcasting should be through proper

Mr Paul Bryan MP, Opposition spokesman on broadcasting before the 1970 General Election. *Sport and General*

community stations, not run by commercial interests, who will only be concerned in maximum profit, but by local broadcasting councils interested in projecting community interests. I am not unhappy about the Conservative threat to introduce commercial radio," added the Minister. "It is just one more reason why the electorate will be supporting Labour at the next General Election."

As the Election approached, more details of the Tory plans were announced. Bryan said that the first thing on his agenda was to commission a comprehensive study to review radio frequencies. There was some speculation over what form the body that would control the new stations would take. *The Times* pointed out that the Conservatives could not really set up an Independent Radio Authority because of the unfortunate choice of initials. Fears were expressed about the future of BBC local radio. Eight VHF local stations were operating in Brighton, Durham, Leeds, Leicester, Merseyside, Nottingham, Sheffield and Stoke on Trent. Further stations at Birmingham, Blackburn, Bristol, Chatham, Derby, Hull, Manchester, Middlesbrough, Newcastle, Oxford, Southampton and London, were planned and due to be on the air by the end of 1970.

In May the Government set up a special Committee under the Chairmanship of Lord Annan, Provost of University College, London, to consider the future of broadcasting again. The Committee was expected to report by 1973. The Conservatives had long been against another comprehensive enquiry into broadcasting. Bryan stated that the major need of broadcasting was for a greater sense of security. He also believed that Annan would not be able to uncover any information not already known.

The Conservatives won the General Election of 1970, but with some help from an unexpected quarter.

At Easter 1970, a multi-coloured radio ship had appeared off the coast, near Frinton, Essex. Transmissions began under the callsign "Radio Northsea International." To begin with, broadcasts were erratic, and the frequency was changed several times. On 15th April, on orders from Minister of Posts and Telecommunications, John Stonehouse, the Post Office started to jam Radio Northsea. This was a somewhat unprecedented course of action for a British Government to take. Not even during the war, when Hitler bombarded Britain with propaganda broadcasts, did the British attempt to interfere with the signals. BBC World Service programmes to countries behind the Iron Curtain have been jammed, but transmissions originating from those countries have never been jammed by the British.

Radio Northsea changed its frequency but each time the Post Office jamming continued. At the beginning of June, one of the owners of the pirate, Edwin Bollier, announced that the station would close on the 19th if a Labour Government was re-elected. The following week the station changed its name to "Radio Caroline International" and launched an intensive anti-Labour Party campaign. During the last few days before the General Election, constant anti-Labour propaganda flowed from the transmitters, and Prime Minister Harold Wilson personally authorised the use of one of the most powerful radio transmitters in Western Europe — a one megawatt (1,000,000 watts) kept near Southend Airport for use in a national emergency.

Labour lost the Election, but the jamming did not stop, as expected by both the pirate's Swiss owners and the listeners throughout the UK. Talks are believed to have taken place, shortly afterwards, between Radio Northsea and the Conservative Government, but to no avail. The jamming continued until Radio Northsea gave up and returned to Holland on 23rd July.

Why the jamming did not stop after the Election has often been debated. But it is possible that certain information was available to the British authorities, at a very high level, about the activities of Radio Northsea's Swiss owners, Mebo of Zurich Ltd., which disturbed them — so much that they have never made this information public. It is unlikely they undertook such a serious measure as "jamming," almost universally condemned in the world of broadcasting, merely to spoil the enjoyment of a few teenage listeners.

Whatever the reasons for the jamming or for Northsea's propaganda, the Conservatives won the Election. It was the first General Election in which the 18-21 age group were able to use their vote. An analysis of the results shows that in the constituencies nearest Radio Northsea, the swing against Labour was greatest. Many constituencies in London and the South East were marginals and a swing of only 1 per cent was needed to change the result. It is possible that Radio Northsea played a decisive role in the Election and may, perhaps, have changed the course of British political history.

The Conservatives were now in power. Former four-minute miler Christopher Chataway was given the post of Minister of Posts and

Telecommunications. He stated the Conservatives would keep their Election promise of introducing local commercial radio. At the Royal Opening of Parliament on the 2nd July 1970, the Queen's Speech confirmed that legislation was to be introduced that proposed local radio stations "under the general supervision of an independent broadcasting authority."

One of Chataway's first moves was to suspend the Committee on Broadcasting under the Chairmanship of Lord Annan. He then invited proposals from various parties for local radio. By this time, nearly four hundred companies had been formed with the intention of applying for licences to operate commercial radio stations. They began to start making themselves known to the Minister. There were two bodies which emerged as the main advocates for commercial radio, the Local Radio Association and Commercial Broadcasting Consultants.

The Local Radio Association, representing 120 companies, proposed a network ultimately of as many as 150 "truly local" stations. The LRA was run by Mr John Gorst, the Conservative MP. He planned stations with a running cost of £60,000 a year. Although the LRA was unwilling to say too much about the content of its programme, it indicated it would be music for 39 minutes in the hour, news five minutes, other speech 10 minutes, advertising six minutes on average and never more than twelve minutes. To the LRA, the threat of competition from the BBC's 11 local VHF stations and the nine more to come was no problem.

"It is our belief that the listening public at the present time is being deceived by the BBC," said John Witney, joint chairman of the LRA.

The other group, Commercial Broadcasting Consultants Limited, was set up in 1966, by Tony Cadman and TV Quizmaster, Hughie Green. One of its first actions, in May 1967 was to commission a study into the feasibility of low-power medium-wave transmissions in the Greater London area. The survey carried out by a Swiss company, Messrs Brown Boveri, was later extended to cover most of the United Kingdom. It showed that, contrary to official opinion, there was still room on the medium waveband for 115 low-power medium frequency stations, all broadcasting in accord with the allocation rulings made by the International Telecommunications Union in Geneva. CBC's findings showed that direct advertising worked out on a basis of 4/- (20p) per thousand, would do little more than cover the basic running costs. Revenue for programming was to be obtained by other means.

CBC's solution was the principle of sponsored programmes produced by and under the control of a licensed contractor. The "patron" would be allowed to insert, say, two minutes of commercials into a programme at defined intervals. After playing his programme over the station of origin, the "patron" could then make it available at no charge to any one or all of the other stations. He would be expected to pay these stations for the commercial time spots according to the station rate card.

Mr Green painted a vivid picture of cities served for 18 to 24 hours a day with programmes of amazing quality. One of his ideas was for a quiz show of such fierce intellect that the prize would be a year's scholarship in the United States. Not only would he play records, he would also feature the entire Hallé Orchestra and award music scholarships to the most gifted of his listeners.

Chataway gathered information from many sources and in October 1970 went off to America to see commercial radio for himself. There he visited a station in New York called Radio Station W.I.N.S. WINS is a 24-hour station that only broadcasts news. It was to be a model for some of his ideas for an all-news station in London.

Early in 1971, Ian Trethowan, managing director of BBC Radio, speaking in a radio discussion, disclosed that the BBC had discovered it would be technically possible for the Government to start commercial radio without losing any of its own services. Although he didn't give away details of the actual frequencies, Trethowan said technical evidence presented by the BBC to the Minister showed it was possible to set up 50 local commercial stations without closing any of the BBC local stations.

On the 29th March, 1971, Chataway's long awaited White Paper *An Alternative Service of Broadcasting* was published. At last the Government's intentions were clear. The main proposal of the White Paper was for a network of about 60 commercial radio stations under the control of the Independent Television Authority (to be re-named the Independent Broadcasting Authority). On medium wave the service would reach 70 per cent of the population in daytime and about 25 per cent at night, because of the behaviour of radio waves after dark. The BBC in the meantime, was to be allowed to continue with its first twenty local stations on VHF, with medium wave support. But the next twenty local radio stations proposed by the BBC would not go ahead.

A system of "rolling" three year contracts, renewable each year, was to be applied to the radio programme companies. This system, Chataway told the House of Commons ". . . will combine strong powers of control for the Authority with prospects of greater security for the programme companies than can be obtained with fixed term contracts."

"The Government's intention," continued Chataway, "is that the stations should combine popular programming with a good service of local news and information. Another major objective of the new service will be to provide an alternative source of national and international news on radio."

The White Paper proposed a central news company that would not necessarily provide complete programmes to the local commercial stations as did Independent Television News. It would, however, be a source of news which "in time would stand comparison with the BBC's and set a standard for the local companies in their treatment of news." Three suggestions were put forward on how the central news company could be organized. One possibility was that Independent Television News might extend its operations. Another was a separate Independent Radio News, organised on similar lines to ITN, and closely collaborating with it. A third possibility would be to provide two competing independent stations in London from the outset, one specialising in music and the other in news. The latter station could then also act as the supplier of national and international news to the local stations around the country.

Mr Ivor Richard, the Opposition spokesman on broadcasting, called the Government's proposals "nothing more than the establishment of sixty pop stations." There was no demand for it, he said. "It is a piece of Conservative theology which is designed to fulfil an ill-considered, half-baked pre-election pledge." Mr Jo Grimond wondered if the new radio contracts would be distributed in the most "extraordinary" way that ITV franchises had been awarded. Reactions came from the many interested parties. Hughie Green, head of Commercial Broadcasting Consultants, was generally delighted with the White Paper. But he criticised the failure to state who would pay for the erection of the commercial stations.

Lord Annan, Chairman of the Committee of Enquiry into the Future of Broadcasting, appointed 10th April, 1974. *Crown Copyright*

"I hope it will not come out of public money," he said. "The taxpayer or ratepayers should not be expected to pay. It should be the people who get the franchise of the stations who pay."

Tory MP, John Gorst, speaking on behalf of the Local Radio Association, said he had reservations about the wide powers of the new IBA which would be given "a fantastic concentration of power." He also claimed that it was regional radio and not local radio.

A consultancy group, Local Radio Services, headed by Philip Waddilove and formed to help franchise seeking groups both apply for licences and run stations, said it was delighted with the White Paper's proposals. However, Waddilove added that he felt that local stations would need to keep the requirements of their audiences uppermost in their minds.

The various pressure groups felt that the Minister's plans did not go far enough. "We are pleased that the Government intends to break the BBC's radio monopoly," said Free Radio Association Chairman, Geoffrey Pearl. "We regret the absence of proposals for national commercial radio. We shall continue to press for a free system of broadcasting."

"The White Paper is too timid, but a step in the right direction," said David Prewitt of the Campaign for Independent Broadcasting. "We feel that the Government has not sufficient confidence in private enterprise and has decided to severely restrict it.

The setting up of an independent broadcasting authority with its overall powers of ownership and finance to control the commercial stations will only dampen any enthusiasm there may be for the system." He added, "It will reduce operators to mere programme contractors."

A third pressure group, the Free Communications Group, gave its views: "Mr Chataway's system is made up of odds and ends of other people's ideas. He has preferred shoddy compromise with existing interested groups to trying to decide what the listener really needs and wants."

The White Paper said that sponsored programmes would not be allowed in the new system and that a heavy load of the detailed planning of the network was laid on the newly-created IBA. More medium frequency channels to accommodate both BBC local radio and commercial radio would be required. The Government would be applying for them under Article 8 of the Copenhagen Convention and Article 9 of the International Telecommunications Union radio regulations. But the exact number of stations and their location was to be decided by the IBA, although the Government expected them to be of different sizes.

When asked by Opposition Leader, Harold Wilson, in the Commons, when the legislation proposed would be forthcoming, Chataway replied: "The legislation would not be in this session, but early in the next."

A few months later, the White Paper came up for discussion in Parliament. Opening the debate, Chataway dismissed complaints that the introduction of commercial radio would debase broadcasting standards.

"Would the cultural standards of the Jimmy Young Show really be lowered?" he asked. "The commercial station would not be able to put out non-stop 'pop' even if they wanted to." But to loud complaints from Labour MP's he said nothing about the control of the stations or their programme content. An Opposition amendment disapproving of the White Paper was later defeated by 247 votes to 214 (a Government majority of 33).

Radio Veronica, the popular Dutch pirate station.　　　　　　　F.R.A.

6 A Sound Act

IT WAS in fact during the next session of Parliament, two days after the Queen's Speech, that the Sound Broadcasting Bill was published. It was sub-titled "an Act to extend the functions of the Independent Television Authority, so as to include the provision of local sound broadcasting services." The Bill consisting simply of twenty pages; thirteen clauses and two schedules confirmed that radio was to be subject to almost exactly the same controls as was commercial television under the Independent Television Authority. Its most obvious feature was that it left all important decisions to the new Authority, which was expected to increase its headquarters staff by about 150. And there were to be Treasury Loans of up to £2 million for the establishing of the network.

The Authority would be required to appoint local advisory committees, and publish certain information from a contractor's application relating to the character of the local sound broadcasts which he proposed to provide if his application were accepted by the Authority.

Clause 6 of the Bill stated that the Authority could not offer a contract to a television contractor within the same area. It also disqualified record companies, music publishers and certain others from holding contracts. Another clause required the Authority to afford newspapers the opportunity in certain circumstances to acquire a shareholding in local radio. Although the Bill was now published, it was a further eight months before it reached the Statute Book.

The number of companies being formed with the intention of applying for licences was running into hundreds. Among the larger companies interested in the field were Beaverbrook Newspapers, Associated Newspapers, Westminster Press, British Lion, Rank, Rediffusion, Granada, Scotia Investments and the William Hill Organisation. Even the Church of England was preparing a bid!

Provisional sites for the first four stations were announced shortly before Christmas 1971, by Minister Chataway. They were to be London, Birmingham, Glasgow and Manchester, and if circumstances were favourable, they would be on the air sometime in 1973. "Another five stations might come into operation a few months later including one in a relatively small town," he added.

The Sound Broadcasting Bill passed its Second Reading in the Commons, but only after two divisions and twenty minutes of near bedlam in the House. Shouting Labour MP's tried to persuade the Speaker, in a barrage of points of order, to postpone further debate on the Bill, after denying Chataway the opportunity to wind up for the Government. Chataway had opened the debate, and according to established procedure, he could only speak a second time with the permission of the House. Without that permission, Mr Francis Pym, Government Chief Whip, called for the closure of the debate. But the Government had its way in the division lobbies and on the second division carried its second reading by a majority of 32 (289 — 257).

The Opposition denounced the Bill as "legislature nonsense" with no real attempt to show a need for commercial radio, and qualified its threat of counteraction if Labour returned to power. Mr Ivor Richard, Labour front bench broadcasting spokesman, said that an in-coming Labour Government would halt the process of establishing commercial radio until a Royal Commission had had opportunity to look at sound and television broadcasting for the 70's and beyond.

"BBC Radio could do with some competition," said Chataway, "not because it is bad, but because I am sure it will benefit from having a competitor by which to measure at least some part of its performance."

"It's a waste of wavelengths," replied Richard, "As far as Britain is concerned, I believe it will result in a trivialisation of the broadcasting media and I am against it."

Later the same month, Conservative MP for Hendon North, John Gorst, published a leaflet through Aims of Industry, entitled "Commercial Radio . . . the Beast of Burden." He criticised the Government's local radio plan and described it as "meagre." He argued that truly local radio would help to preserve and reinforce the individuality of small communities and would offer an outlet to a new category of local advertisers. Chataway's proposed

Christopher Chataway, Minister of Posts and Telecommunications (1970-1972) — the arch-architect of the Sound Broadcasting Bill 1972. *Charles Howard*

"regional" system would do neither and would even tend to force communities into a merging of individuality.

Gorst went on to propose that the existing 20 BBC Local Radio stations should be handed over to commercial interests immediately. He supported the view of the Local Radio Association that it was technically possible for 116 local stations to operate. He dismissed as "groundless" fears that British radio stations would not be economically viable. He foresaw an income of about £50 million a year and suggested that even limited to the 60 stations proposed by the Government, the system is likely to attract £20 million a year.

Parliament, the pamphlet added, should not agree to delegate structural decisions relating to the new services to the IBA without retaining the power to discuss and if necessary reject them.

In December, the Radio Bill began its passage through a standing committee in the Commons. The first day in Committee, discussions were devoted to considering on which days the Committee would meet. The second was centred on the words "independent" and "broadcasting," and the Labour Members monopolised the debate. After five hours deliberation, the Committee had not got beyond Clause 1, Page 1, line 9!

The argument began with a reference to the Concise Oxford Dictionary, as Ben Ford (Lab.) disputed the word "independent." "Independent of what?" he asked, "certainly not the profit motive!" Caerwyn Roderick (Lab.) followed the same line. "If we are talking about independence, then surely it is the BBC that is independent, not the new authority which is proposed."

It was typical of the meetings which followed. Labour MP's tried to defeat the Government on every line. On several occasions they were successful. Rebel Conservative MP, John Gorst, with Labour support won an amendment that would prevent the creation of an "All-news" station in London, servicing the network. They said that stations should be free to rely on existing news agencies for their news and that syndication services should be allowed to develop as in America and Canada. Gorst's amendment meant that a specialist station could not be set up until at least 60 stations existed.

Gorst later proposed amendments that would limit newspapers from buying into local radio. Both he and Wilf Proudfoot (Con.) voted with the Opposition, which resulted in the entire removal of the clause in the Bill relating to local newspapers. But the Government's embarrassment over the defeat was only to be shortlived. They sought to restore the clause to the Bill at the later report stage.

In March 1972, an amusing incident occurred during the Standing Committee's debate on the Bill. In fact it made history in the Palace of Westminster. For the first time in Parliament, a tape recording was used in a debate. An amendment was being discussed which stipulated that "no contract between the Authority and a sound broadcast contractor shall lay down the nature or the amount of music which is to be broadcast . . ." Philip Whitehead, Labour MP for Derby North, attempted to play a part of a cassette recording of a landbased pirate radio station called Radio Jackie. An argument followed as to whether or not it was in order for the Honourable Member to bring the machine into the Chamber.

Mr Ivor Richards (Labour) stated: "I have done some calculations. We commenced the Committee stage of this Bill on the 25th

November 1971. It is now 7th March 1972. We have had 34 sessions and if one takes an average of 2½ hours per session, we have spent approximately 84 hours discussing this Bill. Although my arithmetic is not good, I think that amounts to a total of approximately 67,320 words, which is about two thirds of the length of *War and Peace*. We have done it all orally, we have talked about commercial radio, but never have heard it."

The Chairman accepted the argument and ruled that the cassette could be played. Proudfoot asked if a copyright had been paid for the broadcasting. "If Radio Jackie is prepared to seek me out, I will pay it," replied Whitehead. "I am informed that Radio Jackie has been running for 2½ years on 227 metres medium wave on Sundays, starting at 11 o'clock and ending at 3. It also runs on VHF on 94.4 MHz."

Hansard, the Official Record of all Parliamentary Proceedings, simply states that a "passage of recorded words and music" was then played. Afterwards Whitehead continued, "If those people were transmitting not from the middle of a field on a car battery, but with an acknowledged and recognised transmitter, licensed by the IBA . . . their non-stop pop and disc jockey chatter would be far more popular than any other commercial broadcasting around."

Although Whitehead said he admired Radio Jackie's cheek and pertinacity, he made the point that if the Amendment was carried, there would be no stipulation as to the amount or nature of the music to be broadcast. "We should have at the end of the day," continued Whitehead, "something like the sound I demonstrated." The Amendment was rejected. However, it was the only occasion throughout the Bill's entire passage through Parliament that the Honourable Members heard any example of commercial radio.

At the report stage of the Sound Broadcasting Bill, Chataway, now the Minister for Industrial Development, moved new clauses restoring the right for local newspapers to acquire shareholdings in local radio. He said that it would be contrary to Government policy if the new medium was able to establish a new monopoly by destroying existing local newspapers. But he also introduced a further amendment to ensure that newspapers in the aggregate should not be able to control the system. There were to be safeguards against anybody having too large a share.

The clause provided for newspapers published at intervals of not more than seven days, having a circulation in the area of the radio station. Referring to an Opposition amendment to extend the right of participation to publications published fortnightly, Mr Golding (Labour) said, "The amendment would enable *Private Eye* to compete for the Radio Neasden station!"

The first new clause was approved by 179 − 154 (Government majority 25). The second new clause providing exceptions to the provision for newspaper holding was approved without a division. The following day the Government was able to restore to the Bill its proposal for an "all-news" commercial radio station in London, which had also been deleted at the Committee stage. Chataway wanted a really good almost round-the-clock supply of news, alternative to the BBC. Several Opposition amendments to the Bill were defeated and it was given its third and final reading in the Commons. It was passed 162 − 138, a Government majority of 24.

Chataway, the architect of the Bill, had been moved to another ministerial post. His replacement at the Ministry of Posts and Telecommunications, Sir John Eden, made his first important public statement about radio at the beginning of May, 1972. Speaking at *Tune-in 72*, a London seminar organised by Beaverbrook Commercial Broadcasting, he announced that ten more locations for stations would be announced when the Bill completed its stages through Parliament.

An Opposition attempt to delete the clause relating to newspapers in the Bill was made again at the Committee stage in the House of Lords. But it was rejected, 72 − 47 with a Government majority of 25. No changes to the Bill were made by the Lords and it was passed on the 12th June, 1972. The same day it received the Royal Assent, and became the Sound Broadcasting Act 1972. A month later on 12th July, the Independent Television Authority officially became the Independent Broadcasting Authority.

A few days before, the sites of 21 more commercial radio stations were announced by Sir John Eden. They were split into batches, the first being Bradford, Edinburgh, Ipswich, Liverpool, Nottingham, Plymouth, Portsmouth, Sheffield, Swansea and Tyneside. The second group which would be "likely" to open later comprised of Belfast, Blackburn, Bournemouth, Brighton, Bristol, Cardiff, Coventry, Huddersfield, Leeds, Teeside and Wolverhampton.

Commercial radio was now *in* the air, but not yet *on* the air!

7 The New Authority

UNTIL 1954, all broadcasting in the United Kingdom was provided by the BBC and paid for by members of the public, through the sale of broadcasting receiving licences. In 1954, Parliament authorised the creation of an additional public television service, to be provided by independent television companies and financed through the sale of advertising time.

On the 30th July 1954, the Television Act received its Royal Assent and became law. Five days later the Independent Television Authority was set up by the Postmaster General under the chairmanship of Sir Kenneth Clark, KCB. The Authority consisted of eleven members appointed by the Postmaster General, with the statutory task of providing broadcasting services, including both the provision of the transmitting facilities and the general supervision of programmes.

The ITA advertised for TV programme companies for London, the Midlands and the North. It was not until the 22nd September 1955, that the first broadcasts began in London. The service during the weekdays was provided by Rediffusion Television and at the weekends by Associated Television. The following year independent television expanded to the Midlands and the North of England, where new companies ABC Television and Granada Television were born.

In the early days of independent television, the ITA was frequently criticised about the way it allocated franchises to programme contractors. It was all carried out behind closed doors and details of the applications by both the successful and unsuccessful parties have never been officially disclosed.

On 12th July 1972, the Authority officially became responsible for Independent Local Radio stations and its title changed to the

Independent Broadcasting Authority (IBA). The Sound Broadcasting Act 1972 was later consolidated with the Television Act 1964 in the Independent Broadcasting Authority Act 1973. On the date that the Authority changed its name, Lord Aylestone, then Chairman, announced:

"This is an important day for us. It may prove to be an historic day in the evolution of sound broadcasting in Britain. Today we are properly in business in radio, and we shall get on with the job enthusiastically and as quickly as possible."

The 67 year old former MP for Leicester South West and Leader of the House of Commons, went on to say that each radio programme company would have to respond to the changing needs of the community and build up a close sense of involvement with its listeners. To survive and flourish, the stations would have to provide a popular and acceptable service, but would also be expected to achieve high standards.

Lord Aylestone, Chairman of the IBA from 1967 to 1975. *Barnet Saidman*

"We shall be looking for men and women capable of running radio stations which will be both lively and responsible," continued Lord Aylestone. "We shall be looking for new voices and new ideas as well as solid professionalism. In the next few months, we and the applicants for the first independent local radio stations will be discussing our aims. But they — and we — will be judged by our achievement."

Brian Young, the Director-General, promised that franchises would be awarded with the maximum publicity and openness. Contractors' prospectuses and programming plans were to be made public as soon as stations went on the air. The Authority had taken note of the disquiet after the issuing of the last set of television contracts, when secret applications were published which showed that some companies were broadcasting programmes that had very little resemblence to what they had promised to the ITA.

The Authority performs four basic functions: (i) the selecting and appointing of the programme companies, (ii) the supervision of the programme planning, (iii) the controlling of advertising, and (iv) the transmitting of the programmes. It is aided by a number of advisory committees, including the General Advisory Council and Scottish, Northern Ireland and Welsh Committees. In each ILR area a Local Advisory Committee appointed by the Authority represents as far as possible, the tastes and interests of residents. Assisted by a staff of about 1,300 it attempts to base its policy on its interpretation of the law.

In June 1972, the Authority published the first of series of notes for the guidance of applicants for radio programme contracts and for the information of the general public. The first consisted of the technical arrangements for the new network. The Authority's basic problem was that it had to plan for sixty local stations, but with only a very limited number of channels available. It decided to make use of highly directional Medium Wave transmitting aerials.

This was something new to the UK. Until that time the BBC had used the conventional vertical mast with an omni-directional field — that is to say the signal transmitted was of equal strength in every direction. The proposed directional aerials would consist of a number of radiating masts at specified distances apart. The same radio signal would be fed into each, but with a slight difference in phase. This would have the effect of "focussing" the radio signals into a directional beam. The size of the angle of the beam would be determined by the distances between masts.

Such directional masts have many advantages. They enable transmitters of a lower power to be used, thus reducing capital, operating and maintenance costs. Because the power is focused in one direction only, it enables the same wavelength to be used in other parts of the country and with the minimum of mutual interference. And by controlling the directivity of both medium wave and VHF transmitting aerial systems, it is possible to get a closer match between the VHF and daytime medium wave coverage, than would be possible by other means.

The IBA was later to do a considerable amount of pioneering work in the use of directional aerials, but was also to run into problems in obtaining sites. Because a large area would be required and because several tall masts would have to be built, planning permission was required from the local authorities. Many were reluctant to give permission for these proposed unsightly structures. It was to become a major headache for the Authority in the years to follow.

Independent Local Radio was also to broadcast on the interference-free quality VHF band. The IBA made two important decisions. Firstly, independent radio was to broadcast in stereo from the outset. In 1972, Radio Two was the only station in stereo and only in some parts of the country. The BBC had yet to extend its stereo broadcasts beyond the Midlands and the South East. The new stations would have a major advantage over their competitors, as in many areas the only stereo broadcasting service would be a commercial station.

The second important move was to decide that VHF directional transmitting aerials with simultaneous vertical and horizontal polarisation would be used. The effect of this was to improve VHF reception for listeners using VHF transistor portables or VHF car radios employing vertical "whip" aerials.

From the beginning the Authority made it clear that the long term future of independent radio rested on the VHF transmissions, with medium wave backup being provided only to launch the service and make it a sound financial prospect in the early years. This was partly because of an international re-allocation of medium wave band frequencies due in 1974.

The medium waveband was last re-planned at a conference in 1948 in Copenhagen. Provision was then made for about 400 transmitters in Europe with a total power of about 20,000 watts. Under the 1948 plan, the highest individual power permitted was 150,000 watts. But in 1974, it was estimated that about 1,500 transmitters were in operation, with a total power of nearly 60,000 watts and individual powers of up to 1,500,000 watts. The long overdue International Radio Conference on frequencies commenced in Geneva in October 1974. The outcome of the conference, which is expected to last several years, will determine the eventual fate of commercial and BBC radio on the medium waveband.

The Independent Broadcasting Authority also published guidelines relating to the required composition of the companies applying for radio franchises. In the early stages no company or person would be allowed to play a leading role in more than one local station. Any operators with a holding of more than 20 per cent in a station would not be allowed a significant holding in another. The Authority stated that it was also aiming to secure the widest diversity of "ownership, control and influence among independent local radio companies." Television companies were to be limited to

Lady Plowden DBE, Chairman of the IBA from 1975. *LNA Photos*

shareholdings of no more than 12½ per cent, and foreign interests would not be allowed significant holdings in the new radio stations.

In July, the Authority announced that the first applications for Manchester, Birmingham, Glasgow and the two London stations would be invited in September by means of advertisements in the national and local press. Work was started on finding suitable sites for the transmitters and obtaining planning permission.

The cost of setting up transmitting stations and their subsequent operation was to be borne by the programme contractors. The IBA would charge a rental which would cover all the costs of providing two transmitting stations (medium wave and VHF) and the IBA's repayments on the Government's £2 million loan. It announced the primary rentals at the beginning of October, for the first five independent stations. They were:

Location	(Estimated Population coverage)	1st Year	2nd Year	3rd Year
London-General	(9.2 million)	£315,000	£350,000	£380,000
London-News	(9.2 million)	£185,000	£205,000	£250,000
Manchester	(2.4 million)	£108,000	£120,000	£132,000
Glasgow	(1.9 million)	£ 85,000	£ 95,000	£105,000
Birmingham	(1.7 million)	£ 75,000	£ 85,000	£ 95,000

A proviso added that the rentals were based on current prices and would be variable according to changes in the Index of Retail Prices. The contracts between the Authority and programme contractors reserved the right for the Authority to increase the primary rentals by up to 20 per cent at any time during the second year of operations.

Room for commercial radio on medium wave was made in September 1972 by the BBC. Transmitters putting out Radio 3 programmes on 194 metres were either closed down or switched to 464 metres. Instead of seven wavelengths for Radio 4 throughout England, only four were used: 434, 330, 285, and 261 metres. Also BBC local radio was heard for the first time on medium wave. The stations had previously operated only on VHF and had only a limited audience. All but six now had the medium wave back-up, promised two years earlier by Chataway.

The race then started for the contracts for the commercial radio franchises. On the 4th October, advertisements inviting applicants appeared in the *Times,* the *Telegraph,* and several other national and local newspapers. Immediately the papers were full of speculation over who would be applying for the franchises. Among the groups were well known names such as Hughie Green, Lord Willis, Lord Mancroft, Peter Hall, Bryan Forbes and Ned Sherrin.

The contender longest in the field appeared to be Wigmore Broadcasting, a company registered in 1960 by Ian Hunter, the concert agent and festival impresario but now associated with the name of Hughie Green. He claimed to have spent £45,000 on extensive research into the financial background of commercial radio. His plans for a round-the-clock London station included music, drama, quizzes and other entertainment. Conservative peer, Lord Mancroft, was Chairman of Wigmore Broadcasting.

Well-known broadcasting names were also connected with Network Broadcasting, also contending for the entertainment station. At its head was Chairman, Lord Ted Willis, creator of *Dixon of Dock Green* and with him three former BBC men, Tony Smith and Neil ffrench-Blake, respectively ex-editor and ex-producer of *24 Hours,* and Ned Sherrin who produced *That Was The Week That Was.* Like Hughie Green's group, Network Broadcasting was planning a 24-hour station, but with particular emphasis on offering "access" to listeners.

Two experienced operators in the commercial radio field, John Witney and Philip Waddilove, were the prime movers in forming Local Radio Services. The two had been founder members of the Local Radio Association. LRS had links with Canadian radio and had the backing of the Robert Stigwood Organisation. Artists in Radio was the title adopted by a group headed by Peter Hall, director-designate of the National Theatre and Michael Kustow, former director of the Institute of Contemporary Arts. Others involved included freelance TV producer John Costello and former public relations officer of the Beatles, Derek Taylor. Their backers included Watneys, the brewers.

During the day, Artists in Radio would go after the mass radio audience, but devote evening programmes to specialised minority interests such as further education and the arts. Cultural ambitions rather than commercial were behind another group, City Sounds, headed by former Labour Minister, Sir Kenneth Younger, with broadcaster Bryan Magee, Prof. Frank Kermode, and literary agent Michael Sissons. It planned to go for the "Under 40 educated London market," rather than a mass audience.

John Thompson, Director of Radio, IBA.　　　　　　　*Auguste Photographics*

Television companies were also interested in the race. Robert Walker, a thirty-nine year-old Australian, headed an application on behalf of ATV. Former holders of the London ITV franchise, Rediffusion, were planning to bid for both the London and Manchester radio franchises. Rediffusion owned 13 overseas commercial stations and two of them, in Jamaica and Malta, were managed by their chief radio executive, Graham Binns.

Theatrical names were involved in another bidder, Capital Radio. The group, formed two years earlier by a dentist from Weybridge, Barclay Barclay-White included Bryan Forbes, Richard Attenborough, Peter Saunders the impresario, and George Martin, the former Beatles' recording manager. Capital's programming according to Barclay-White would be "commercial radio with a conscience," catering for the mass audience during the day and mounting programmes for minorities, especially the old and lonely, in the evenings.

Two newspaper groups also proclaimed their interests. Associated Newspapers, publishers of the *Daily Mail,* formed Associated Independent Radio Services (Air Services) and Beaverbrook Newspapers, publishers of the *Daily Express,* formed Beaverbrook Broadcasting. Ex-pirates were involved in both. Former sales manager of Radio Caroline between 1966 and 1968, Terry Bate headed Beaverbrook's group. Although British, his career until that time had been completely in Canadian radio. The head of Radio London, Caroline's rival in the sixties, was Philip Birch. He was the chief executive of the Air Services' group and, like Bate, his advertising and radio experience was gained on the other side of the Atlantic. Also involved in AIR were David Bassett, a producer of Canadian telephone programmes and former Radio 270 deejay, Bob Snyder.

Many other smaller groups were said to be interested in the regions, and there was some speculation that the International Broadcasting Company would be applying. For several years the company, that had once produced commercial radio programmes before the war, had been run by George Clouston, the musician and Eric Robinson, the television conductor, as a recording studio.

8th December 1972, was the closing date for applications, and in accordance with the Sound Broadcasting Act 1972, the Authority announced the number of applications received. The number of bids for the London General contract was 8, London News 5, Birmingham 4, Glasgow 4 and Manchester 3. There was obviously some merging and juggling of companies shortly before the closing date. And there was more to follow later.

Meanwhile the IBA had started test transmissions. Because it had been under Government pressure to rush commercial radio through before the end of the Parliamentary session, the Authority had been unable to provide adequate transmitting facilities in London. It had been partly frustrated by the refusal of several Labour controlled local authorities to the north of London, in granting planning permission for aerial masts. Instead medium wave broadcasts were to originate from a wire aerial strung between the two chimneys of London Transport's Lots Road power station in Fulham. It soon gained a nickname of "Radio Clothesline."

Two temporary wavelengths were allocated for use from Lots Road, — 417 metres and 539 metres. But shortly after tests started, a Dutch pirate station suddenly changed its wavelength. The popular Radio Veronica had been broadcasting for ten years on 192 metres, but because of increasing interference in Holland from a Swiss station, switched to 539. There was little that the IBA could do about the situation, and for a while it received a large number of complaints from British fans of Veronica.

Because of the use of the temporary transmitting stations, the London catchment area was seriously over-estimated. The various consortia was only told of this after they had put in their applications. It was also learned that the estimate of VHF population coverage at 9.1 million was over by some 660,000. In a letter the Authority said the "original estimate did not represent the guaranteed coverage or any contractual commitment by the Authority." That was in case anyone was considering suing the IBA.

A further confidential letter of 9th January, 1973, from the IBA to the consortia awaiting interviews said: "The purpose of this note is to give information to reduce the need for discussions to take place at the interview on technical matters." It acknowledged that the technical matters were "of considerable concern to applicants" but went on to say that the Authority didn't know the answers itself, so there was no point in talking about them!

The concern among the consortia was that Radio Clothesline would have an audience of only two thirds of that originally envisaged.

Meanwhile the high rental costs had put off some investors. In Birmingham, merchant bankers Singer and Friedlander involved in a partnership group called Radio Brum, were shocked by the £75,000 annual rental. They had already made some calculations based on a much lower rental. Faced with the IBA's figures, they estimated that the potential profit would be halved. They backed off and made way for Eric Morley of Mecca.

One of the most outspoken personalities in the big commercial debate backed out shortly before the closing date for applications. Hughie Green and his consortium decided not to bid for the London General franchise.

"Only the people with fantastic incomes can afford it," declared Green. "You're paying out 30 per cent of your money in copyright charges and rent to the IBA even before you've got four walls; before you've even paid the tea girl!"

His view was that mixed bag advertising spots made little impact on a radio audience, which usually listens with only half an ear while driving or ironing. His alternative of sponsored programming which big national advertisers would find more attractive, was forbidden by the Act, because of the effect sponsorship might have on editorial content. Green also thought the whole process of paying the IBA to build and operate the transmitters was ridiculous. Over three years the total rent for the London General station came to £1,000,000.

"Why do it that way at all," asked Green, "we could have borrowed the money and built our own transmitter. Allowing for depreciation it would cost £700,000 and that's doing it rich. If you're kicked out after three years then at least you'd have an asset. Now you're being asked to pay for something which isn't yours and never will be."

A special selection procedure was devised by the IBA during the early days, which it maintained for all the franchises. The first stage after the closing date for applications, consisted of a study of the situation in each contract area. Outside London, it was carried out by a group of IBA members and staff acting in conjunction with the Authority's Regional Officer. This group held discussions with applicants. Next, the full Authority interviewed in London those applicants who were invited, in the light of the local studies, to come forward to the latter stage of the selection process. The whole selection process took about three months.

Eventually the winners of the first franchises were announced. On the 8th February 1973, the Authority issued the following statement:

"The IBA, after full consideration of the five applications for the London Radio News franchise and of eight applications for the London General Radio franchise, proposes to offer the news contract to the London Broadcasting Company (Chairman – Sir Charles Trinder) and the general contract to Capital Radio (Chairman – Richard Attenborough) subject to certain conditions and further detailed discussion.

"It is considering with these two companies the best way of incorporating certain other elements (including some London newspaper interests) in the groups with which the Authority will sign contracts.

"The final composition of the successful contracting companies will be announced as soon as possible."

The following month the names of the successful contenders outside London were announced. The Birmingham ILR franchise would go to Birmingham Broadcasting Limited, the Manchester franchise to Greater Manchester Independent Radio Group and the Glasgow franchise to Radio Clyde Limited.

Immediately the two London companies named by the Authority were flooded with letters and telephone calls from people seeking jobs. Most of the enquiries were from would-be disc jockeys. But before Capital Radio could consider them, it had to appoint five key executives. Some of Capital's unsuccessful rivals, who were able to name experienced executives in their applications, found it odd that the franchise should go to a group which would have to start the senior staff side from scratch.

"We felt that only a company which already had a franchise to operate could begin recruiting staff on a realistic basis," explained acting Chief Executive Michael Flint, "especially when so many potential candidates are with other groups or with the BBC."

Four interests had come together to form the Capital group: Barclay Barclay-White, the Weybridge dentist who started it; Rediffusion; the *Observer* newspaper and Local News of London, a group controlling 122 local newspapers. None of the companies held a controlling interest.

Meanwhile, the all news station, the London Broadcasting Company, was preparing to start broadcasts. It derived its history from a circle of city businessmen. Roland Freeman, a public relations consultant, formed a consortium called Radio Barbican in 1970, with the backing of Charterhouse Securities and the *Financial Times*. They had originally hoped for six radio stations in London and had visions of a specialist station — a financial news service.

But when it became obvious that there would be only two stations, they decided to go for the "all-news" franchise. They ran across print journalist and author Adrian Ball, who some years earlier had formed a dummy company called London Broadcasting.

Later they attracted the interest of Selkirk Communications Ltd. — a Canadian commercial broadcasting company. They won the franchise after the IBA had suggested they offer a shareholding to two of the unsuccessful bidders — City Sounds and Associated Newspapers.

In June 1973, as the first two commercial radio stations were preparing to go on the air, there came news that the Channel Islands might get a commercial radio station. Like the Isle of Man, the tiny islands close to the French coast felt they ought to have their own local radio. Plans for a station on the Islands came to a halt in September 1970 when the Guernsey States agreed in principle to a station, but the Jersey States referred it back to the Broadcasting Committee. The president of the Guernsey Post Office Board, Conseiller Peppino Santangelo, had been responsible for studying local radio. He said he could not proceed unless Jersey came into line with Guernsey.

Eventually the two States agreed and during the summer of 1973, announced that a joint application would be put into the British Government for a medium wave band frequency for use on the Islands. Talks took place, but no further developments occurred. However, it is understood the matter is still under consideration by the Channel Islands.

As everyone was preparing for the start of LBC and Capital Radio, a full page advertisement appeared in the national press. Its headline declared: "Owing to an oversight commercial radio will not be starting in October." It had been placed by Radio Luxembourg who very rightly pointed out that Britain was not about to get its first commercial radio service. Luxembourg had been around for a very long time and claimed a 12.5 million strong audience, all over Britain. Proudly, it referred to itself as "Britain's one and only national commercial radio station and Britain's most experienced commercial radio station."

The two London stations opened in October and were soon followed by the stations in Glasgow, Birmingham and Manchester. The IBA continued its process of advertising for applicants for different areas and after due consideration awarded franchises. Many of the names involved in unsuccessful bids for the first five franchises started to pop up in other parts of the country.

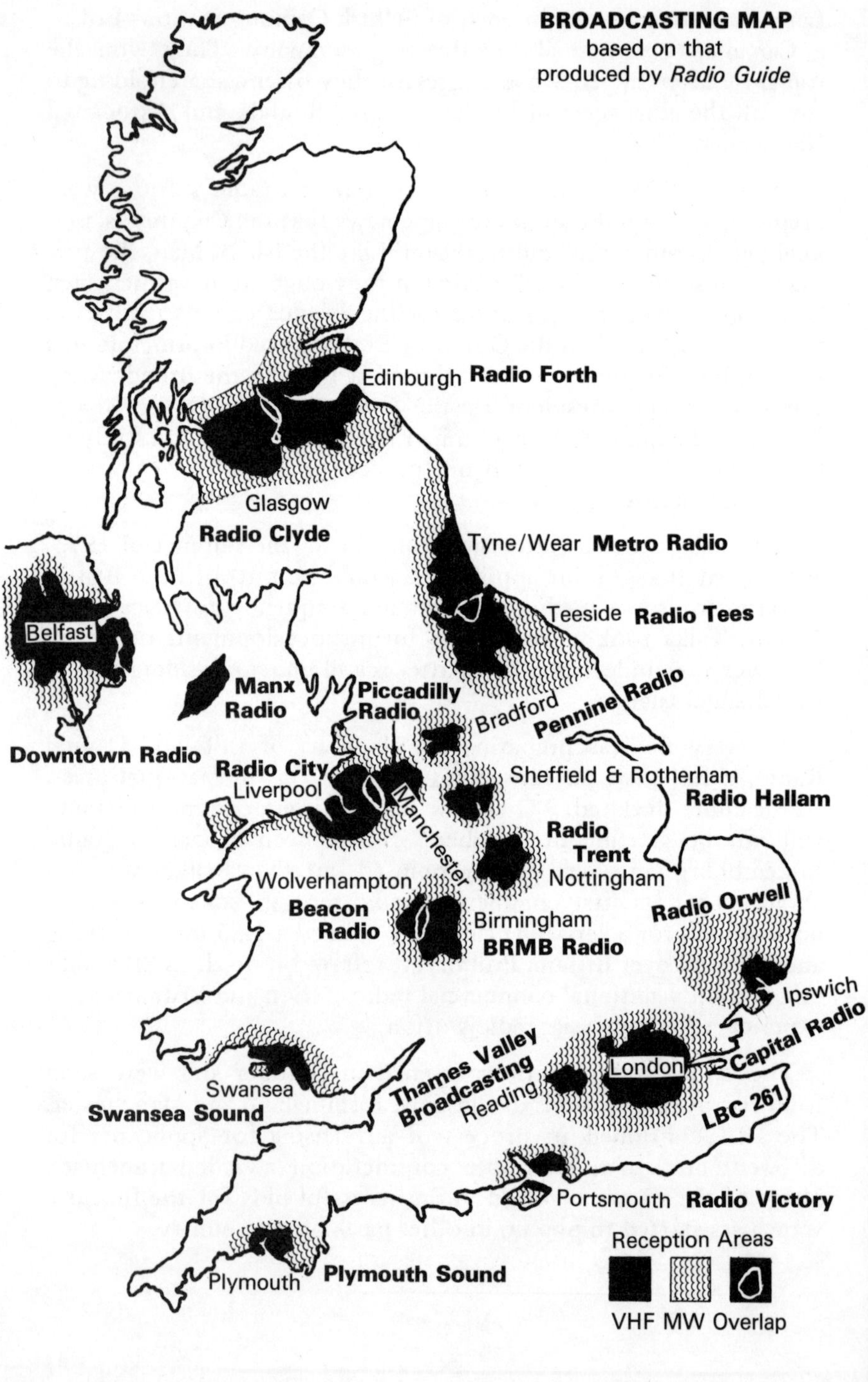
BROADCASTING MAP
based on that
produced by Radio Guide
Edinburgh Radio Forth
Glasgow
Radio Clyde
Tyne/Wear Metro Radio
Teeside Radio Tees
Belfast
Manx Radio
Piccadilly Radio
Bradford
Pennine Radio
Downtown Radio
Radio City
Liverpool
Manchester
Sheffield & Rotherham
Radio Hallam
Radio Trent
Nottingham
Wolverhampton
Beacon Radio
Birmingham
BRMB Radio
Radio Orwell
Ipswich
Capital Radio
London
Thames Valley Broadcasting
Reading
LBC 261
Swansea
Swansea Sound
Portsmouth Radio Victory
Plymouth
Plymouth Sound
Reception Areas
VHF MW Overlap

8 The Independent Local Radio Stations

AS EACH ILR station is independent of every other station, and as they all have identities of their own, they will all be dealt with separately. The following stations are not set out either in size or alphabetically, but in chronological order.

Before reading this chapter, it should be explained that the predicted population coverage figures are those issued by the IBA. They are based on a defined reception area in which the received VHF signal is above a specified strength (1 mv/metre). Within this area satisfactory reception of the stereo broadcasts can be heard. However, the medium wave signal can be heard outside this area, especially at night. Under freak conditions, medium wave signals can travel many hundreds of miles. Swansea Sound can often be heard early in the mornings in London, whereas Radio Tees is frequently monitored in Plymouth.

The ILR companies refer to a larger reception area, which they call the marketing area, or the medium wave reception area. The total predicted cover of ILR, based on the IBA VHF areas is 25,515,000 or 46 per cent of the population of the British Isles. The estimated medium wave coverage of the population, based on the companies' marketing areas, is 40 million (72.1 per cent of the UK population).

The map of the UK showing both the reception areas for the VHF and the medium wave signals of each station was produced by *Radio Guide,* the monthly magazine all about radio.

LONDON BROADCASTING.

Serving Greater London and the South East from transmitters in North and South London.

First transmission: 8th October 1973.

Estimated Population: 8,500,000.

On a cold and wet October morning in 1973, a strangely clad figure with a bell walked through the streets of London's boroughs shouting out a message. The man was Britain's champion town crier with a special announcement. At about the same time a thousand pigeons were released into London's sky, and as the city was beginning to wake, just a few seconds before 6 a.m., engineer Howard Yentis opened the controls of a brand new radio studio just off Fleet Street. Then, a 30-second signature tune and the words "This is London Broadcasting, the news and information voice of independent radio," marked the birth of Britain's first local commercial radio station.

Apart from some first-morning stuttering and imperfect links, the first day of London Broadcasting Company programmes was relatively trouble free. The first words were spoken by David Jessel, previously with the BBC Television programme *Midweek* who was now a regular presenter of LBC's breakfast segment, *The Morning*

Janet Street-Porter with Paul Callan in the early days of the London Broadcasting Company. *IP Studios*

Show. A few minutes later followed the first commercial. It was for Bird's Eye Fish Fingers.

News bulletins at the top of the hour were read in the Australian tones of Ken Guy and at the half hour by Josephine Bacon. The all-news radio station was born in the middle of the outbreak of the Middle East war and on the day Prime Minister Edward Heath announced his controversial Phase Three policies. The early voice reports about the war were in strong American accents, as the new station did not have any foreign correspondents of its own. Instead it relied on agencies. In the breakfast programme such reports came from Moscow, New York, Beirut and the Golan Heights.

Two commercials — one for an airline and another for a furniture company — were heard at the same time, and a first attempt to go to the A.A. Operations Centre at Stanmore was greeted with silence. "I expect it was like this in the BBC's early days," said David Jessel.

At 9 a.m. Jessel signed off to make way for *Two in the Morning*, which, according to the programme schedule handout, would feature "the flavour of life in London everywhere, the bits radio so often misses out," and be introduced by Paul Callan and Janet Street-Porter. The sharp Etonian and suave accent of Paul Callan contrasted with the fruity and weirdly polished Cockney accent of Miss Street-Porter.

The first regular phone-in programme *Open Line* followed at noon. The first guest on the show, Michael Cudlip, the Chief Editor, found himself having to defend the choice of Janet Street-Porter for the 9 — 12 show. He described her as a 6ft. 5in. tall redhead. "She frightens the life out of us all; she is a very nice lady," said Cudlip. One listener spoke of "the drivel this woman talks" and suggested that many in the audience would not understand her until she had taken elocution lessons. Cudlip replied that although she was a little hard to understand, there were many people in London who talked just like what she did! However, it didn't take up the point of the caller that she did not talk very intelligently when she was intelligible. Next day on the show she was still there talking about a bacon sandwich.

A few days later, the station claimed that it had been overwhelmed by the fantastic public response to its phone-in programmes. All ten lines reserved for the phone-ins had been jammed without a break since the opening.

"In the first 100 hours on the air, the station's staff spoke to, or played recorded messages to, more than 8,000 people," said a spokesman. "Of these 8,000 it was possible to get roughly one in ten of the callers on the air. The pressure of calls for 24 hours a day, suggests to experienced engineers that at least 20,000 people must have been trying to call the station with comments on news and matters of contemporary interest."

The station said that it had intended to take out large advertisements in the evening's newspapers to make a public apology to the thousands unable to get on the air. The space was not available so tens of thousands of handbills were printed and handed out to home-going commuters at underground stationa. The handbill thanked Londoners for their "astonishing response" to the phone-in programmes and promised: "Believe us, your turn will come (even if, like Andre Previn, it's 3.15 in the morning)."

The *Daily Mail* carried out a special news analysis on "The Day Radio Was Born." A number of listeners were asked their views on the new radio station. Sheila Wood, a dress designer from Holland-on-Sea, Essex, said: "The news is disjointed, doesn't flow, carries no weight or conviction as important information, can't hold a candle to the BBC. And as soon as names like Mary Quant were interviewed – forget it. It's the same old stuff being served up in the same way."

Another listener, Andrea Newman, an author in her 30's living in Chelsea, added: "I tuned in and thought I was in America. I don't mind watching commercials because they're pretty, they're amusing. But they're so irritating to listen to. And I don't like being bombarded with news all the time."

Within a few days, London Broadcasting had lost most of its "er-sorries," and Janet Street-Porter with her ear-piercing Fulham whine instantly became the "Woman London Loved to Hate." Although there was not an enormous amount of advertising, there was enough for London Broadcasting to call itself a commercial radio station. On the surface, all appeared well, but inside it wasn't quite the same.

The station was run mainly by journalists but the staff included a lot of broadcasters, many from the BBC – both with very

Adrian Love, son of the musician, Geoff Love, and presenter of Britain's first all night phone in programme on London Broadcasting.

different attitudes. Some of the journalists loftily assumed that technical problems could be easily overcome. While the broadcasters, used to the impeccable, almost regimental standards of the BBC, were in a state of despair. Towards the end of October, reports started to filter out from the Gough Square studio and news room complex of staff having to work long hours, and several collapsing through overwork, and exhaustion.

The National Union of Journalists branch at the radio station held its first meeting in October. The only demands it made were for coat hooks, a shower and a canteen. However, the following month, they put in for salary increases of up to £700 to bring the minimum up to £2,500.

London Broadcasting's board suddenly realised that the cost of operating a 24 hours a day seven days a week, all-talk radio station, was proving to be more than expected.

After only a month on the air, the board decided to put a freeze on all recruitment for three months, although the station was well understaffed. Some people were said to be working a 70 to 80 hour

BUT WHAT IF YOU DON'T THINK RADIO ONE IS WONDERFUL?

The 'Oohjahs' have shot to the top of the 'Terrific Twenty' again. Mrs Beatty Lamb is celebrating her silver wedding anniversary in Warrington. And you're wondering if there shouldn't be something a little more stimulating on your radio.

'A brand new kind of old-fashioned radio.'

On October 8th, radio could just become the vital, entertaining, and engrossing medium it was in the days before musical wallpaper became the style.

Tune-in to 417 metres Medium wave, 97.3 metres VHF or 719 kHz and you'll be witnessing the birth pangs of a new kind of radio station. A station with the old kind of radio ideals.

'Read the newspaper with your eyes closed.'

London Broadcasting is first and foremost a communications station A cross between a newspaper with a mouth and a radio with ears.

It's exclusively for Londoners. But its news net spans the globe. If a man swallows a rabbit in Walthamstow we'll have a gulp by gulp commentary; if a man swallows his pride in Washington, the facts will be there in the same thorough, but palatable, style.

'We never close.'

News is happening 24 hours a day. We'll be there 24 hours a day telling you about it. With more time we'll be able to dig deeper, think further, report fuller. Whenever you tune-in a news bulletin will never be more than 20 minutes away.

'Don't just sit there, say something.'

We're creating our radio station as a 'two-way' affair. There'll be 'Openline' programmes, every day, on things as varied as cookery and black magic.

You can ring us 24 hours a day with comments and criticisms.

We're not looking for people who like the sound of their own voices, we believe there are too many important issues for chat shows. But anyone with a genuine gripe, a fervent interest or good advice, on anything that comes up, will be given plenty of opportunity to make their feelings known.

Our way to success is through variety guided by intelligence. Through honesty combined with a sense of humour. In short, our way to success is through people like you.

417·LONDON BROADCASTING

Tune in on 417 metres, 719 kHz and VHF 97·3. You've never heard anything like it.

week. Already rumours were circulating suggesting that LBC was heading for a cash crisis.

When the station began broadcasting in October, it promised that the only music to be heard on the air would be in the commercial spots. But on 12th November 1973, realising it could not sustain an all-speech output 24 hours a day, without severely straining its resources and staff, it introduced a music programme. A major three hour long arts programme which included reviews of records — both classical and pop — replaced an evening news magazine and cut two hours off the phone-in show, *Nightline*.

A week later there was further re-organisation of the programmes. The controversial Janet Street-Porter and Paul Callan programme was shortened by one hour to make way for a major news programme, *London At One*. Three days after the start of the new show, the journalists told the management that unless they took on extra staff, they would black the programme. The management agreed to put one full-time producer on to *London At One*.

Meanwhile, the financial situation of the radio station seemed to be getting worse, although the management denied it. Michael Levete, Managing Director, insisted that "although the revenue is a little less than was forecast and costs are a little higher, there is no crisis. We never expected to make any taxable profits until 1976."

When journalists met management again in December to make more demands for staff for *London At One,* they were told the station was reviewing its format and programme content and that some redundancies were likely. It appeared that the review was a result of the Board of Directors' awareness that its overheads were too high. Also London Broadcasting was not securing very much advertising revenue.

On 10th December, the NUJ Chapel (official Union branch) visited the Independent Broadcasting Authority and asked them to investigate the running of London Broadcasting and refuse to discuss redundancies while the present management existed. But the Authority refused to intervene. The following day Labour MP's joined the journalists in calling for an IBA inquiry into the running of the radio station.

Just five days before Christmas, and only eleven weeks after the station's opening, three directors of the company resigned in a boardroom re-shuffle. Out went Sir Charles Trinder, Chairman,

Michael Levete, Managing Director, and Michael Cudlip, Chief Editor. The decision that the three directors should resign was made at an emergency meeting of the board at which the whole future of the station was examined. Sir Gordon Newton, a former Editor of the *Financial Times,* became non-executive Chairman. A few weeks later in the New Year, Canadian Bill Hutton was appointed Chief Executive of the crisis ridden news station. Hutton had spent most of his working life in radio journalism, and had been closely associated with London Broadcasting from its formative days, as a consultant, and helped draw up the franchise application.

"I have always believed in the concept of a news and information service," said Hutton. "Nothing that has happened in London Broadcasting's brief history has diminished my confidence in the station."

However, as the new man took over, the man whose voice launched commercial radio in Britain, resigned. David Jessel announced he would be departing from the station in the near future. He was one of the few experienced broadcasters that LBC had, joining the station after working for the BBC on *World At One, Twenty Four Hours* and *Late Night Line Up.*

"I do not regret having left the BBC," explained Jessel. "I thought that LBC was going to do something really new but as soon as I arrived I realised how short of resources the station was. We did our best to produce a sort of mini-*Today,* but it can't be done with such an absurd budget."

Later, in an article written by Jessel in the *New Statesman,* he revealed that the opening announcement of the station — "It's six o'clock in the morning, Monday October the Eighth. Welcome to London Broadcasting, the news and information voice of commercial radio" — was in fact recorded a few days previously. The tape underwent one minor modification . . . "the word "commercial" was replaced by an equally misleading euphemism, "independent." It was a wise substitution. "It will be some time before LBC is a commercial proposition," wrote Jessel.

Morale improved at the station towards the end of January 1974, when a National Opinion Poll survey revealed that over a million people were listening to the news station each week. The average weekday audience was 385,000 a day, falling to 310,000 at the weekends. Of the people who listened to LBC, 82 per cent said they liked the news output and virtually the same, 81 per cent liked the overall programming of the station.

A new programming format was put to the staff by Bill Hutton at the end of the month. He said he would not take his new plans to the IBA for approval until there had been full consultation with the staff. The acute financial difficulties of the station and the need to make changes as quickly as possible were explained by Hutton at a meeting of the staff. But the following day the staff rejected the revamped programming and also management demands for eighteen redundancies. They said the proposals were incompatible with the station's prospectus and they refused to discuss programme changes until a Chief Editor was appointed.

The proposed line-up would mean more news and information until 7 p.m. then two hours music and another three hours information to midnight. The news programmes would be in 30-minute blocks with five minutes of news and then segments on weather, traffic and other material.

After a further two months negotiations between LBC's management, the unions and the IBA, finally a solution was reached. A News Editor, ex-BBC editor of Radio 4's *Today* programme, Marshall Stewart, was also appointed. On 4th March 1974, the new programmes came into operation. *The Morning Show* was re-titled *AM* and hosted by Alan MacKenzie and Douglas Cameron (who had just joined the station from the *Today* programme). *Two in the Morning* show with Paul Callan and Janet Street-Porter was axed, and in its place came George Gale's *Open Line*. Marshall Stewart, announcing the new tighter format, said there would be a new two hour lunch-time programme *Newsday*.

"*Newsday* is a major step forward because it will allow for more varied coverage of Greater London affairs, personalities on the London scene, as well as an extension of the national and international news."

London Broadcasting's income is derived from two sources — advertising revenue and the money that other ILR stations are required to pay to LBC for the Independent Radio News Service. By April 1974, Independent Radio News was beginning to grow out of the old LBC/IRN nucleus. Four other stations (Capital Radio, Radio Clyde, BRMB Radio and Piccadilly Radio) were now on the air and some re-organisation of IRN as a news gathering agency was required. IRN first got itself together in its own right at the General Election in February, and moved into a position where it was supplying news to LBC and the other stations to use as they thought fit. The news area at LBC was rebuilt with IRN working from a hexagonal control desk in the middle of the room. A similar shaped desk used by LBC for London news gathering was nearby. Ron Onions, Head of News at Capital Radio, became Editor of Independent Radio News.

Throughout most of 1974, "LBC 417" as it had become known, showed general signs of improvement. A traffic helicopter was introduced in April. From 7 a.m. to 9 a.m. every weekday morning in LBC's *AM* show, the 'copter hovered over the capital reporting live the up-to-date road situation. The Hughes 300C helicopter cost LBC £32 per flying hour. "We are a news and information service and this is really the only way to cover the traffic properly," said an LBC spokesman.

But it was not long before the company ran into financial problems and trouble with the unions again. In August Bill Hutton, the Chief Executive, threatened to close the station down immediately and put the company into the hands of the liquidators, because of a staff revolt over a station promotion. They claimed it was knocking the BBC. The threat by Hutton infuriated the IBA. Hutton said that unless the contentious promotional tape was broadcast by 6.05 that evening, he would close down the station. The crisis came just one day after the station was twice blacked off the air because of a dispute with ACTT union (the sound engineers' union). Under some pressure from the IBA — who had been trying to negotiate a peace settlement with the union — Hutton agreed to put out the tape just twice more.

John Thompson the IBA's Director of Radio, had been that week lobbying a new Labour Government that was threatening to freeze further expansion of commercial radio. His main argument was that unless more stations were allowed to go on, both LBC and, more importantly, its sister Independent Radio News might be forced to close down. Referring to the LBC rumpus, Thompson said, "It was an incident that I could well have done without."

A pay row hit the station again the following February. For two and a half hours, the twelve independent local radio stations that were by then broadcasting, were without the normal IRN news service. The National Union of Journalists called a chapel (official Union branch) meeting following a dispute over a confidential letter sent to the LBC staff by Hutton, rejecting wage claims. He also spoke of the need to cut staff and broadcasting hours. "It is now clear," he wrote, "that LBC and IRN will have to survive on a smaller, skilled staff."

The following month, the IBA launched a rescue operation to help the station out of its financial crisis. It had been estimated that LBC was losing money at the rate of £100,000 a month. The Authority agreed to waive the rental of £168,000 for nine months up to September, which the station was required to pay for the use of the transmitters. It also agreed to a restructuring of programmes so as to reduce running costs. But despite the assistance, the station was still forced to make one third of its 180 staff redundant. The cut had been agreed with the NUJ. For the journalists remaining, there was to be a pay rise of twenty per cent.

The main economies on programming were made by dropping the all-night phone-in programme and the specialist magazine programmes which were broadcast in the late evenings. The *Night Line* programme was brought forward to nine in the evening, with the station closing down at midnight. However, although there were no programmes in the small hours, the news operation did not stop, as IRN still had to feed to the other ILR stations — some of which are 24 hour operations. So throughout the night a test tone was interrupted on the hour for a three minute bulletin.

The Radio Car and Traffic Helicopter.

The weekday pattern concentrated on news and information for the London area between 6 a.m. and 7.30 p.m. Between 7.30 p.m. and 9 p.m. there were programmes of popular classical music, interspersed only by the regular news bulletins.

So, during its first two years, Britain's first independent local radio service has been plagued with union disputes — although not wholly unjustified — and financial problems. Some of the trouble has been caused by initial bad planning and early mis-management. But the signs are that it is now pulling out of its turbulent past. Audience ratings are currently around the million per week figure, and there is still some interest from the advertising industry. As more stations open up, Independent Radio News receives more money from subscribers. They pay on the basis of about £20 per thousand listeners, so when all nineteen Independent Local Radio stations are operating, LBC will be receiving over half a million pounds a year. That sort of figure will help to make LBC and IRN into a viable concern.

CAPITAL RADIO.
Serving Greater London and the South East from transmitters in North and South London.
First transmission: 16th October 1973.
Estimated Population Coverage: 8,500,000.

The man who started Capital Radio was a man named Barclay Barclay-White, a Weybridge dentist. In 1970, he'd taken his family to a holiday house where he accidentally listened to the pirate station, Radio Northsea, with his daughters, then 20 and 18, and their boy friends. "We knew," he said, "that commercial radio would come if the Conservatives won the Election. And they pressed me to put up some money to help them apply for the franchise."

It was all semi-serious, but Barclay-White was sufficiently enthused to take a trip to the States to investigate the financing of local radio. "As a small boy," he continued, "I'd had a yearning to be connected with show business. I thought how marvellous to believe in something, and then see it succeed on the first night." He approached his neighbour, Brian Forbes, the film director, and persuaded him to join his infant Capital Radio Company. Forbes suggested he contact a friend, Richard Attenborough, so Barclay-White took another day off from his dental practice and persuaded Attenborough to be linked loosely with the project. He then linked his little company in equal partnership with Rediffusion, The *Observer* and Local News of London. He also insisted the name should remain Capital Radio, "although I had to defend it constantly against people who thought it would be taken as meaning money. But I was determined to go all out for the London franchise, and what name could be more appropriate?" Later George Martin and TV and radio presenter, David Jacobs, joined in.

Seven other consortia applied for the London franchise when it was advertised by the IBA. One of the other companies was Network Broadcasting headed by Lord Ted Willis and including Ned Sherrin. Their application was a glossy enormous £50,000 worth of research, accountancy, engineering, cartography and imagination. They had over £1 million worth of capital lined up. In the first year of operation, they hoped to gross £7 millions.

According to a report in the Magazine, *Time Out,* by Mark Hosenball in 1973, the IBA was impressed by Network's application. A few days after the final interview, Lord Ted Willis was invited to the IBA's headquarters in Knightsbridge, by Director-General Brian Young, and was told that another application had struck the IBA's fancy. Before he left, he was handed a piece of paper with Richard Attenborough's name and phone number on it.

Apparently Attenborough who was fronting the Capital Radio application, received similar treatment at the Authority on the same day, complete with a slip of paper. The IBA felt Network and Capital should merge, and a few days later Attenborough and Willis met to discuss the possibilities of a merger. By all accounts Willis offered Attenborough a 40 per cent share of Network. But the board of Capital did not want to be taken over, so turned the offer down. The IBA was notified, and a few days later, so the story goes, Willis was soaking in his bath, when his wife brought him an IBA envelope containing notification that Capital Radio had won the contract.

The Authority obviously will never confirm whether or not the *Time Out* report was correct or not. But it is difficult to see what Capital had that Network didn't. Capital had no staff line-up at all, whereas Network had a programme controller — and nearly twenty programmers at the ready. Network is reported as having a complete programme blueprint with detailed scheduling and programme descriptions, but Capital Radio's published programme intentions from the application are incredibly vague and non-committal. The franchise may have been awarded to Capital because of its financial backing, and because the IBA considered Network's projections a bit extravagant. In any case the franchise went to Capital, although Lord Willis was later offered a shareholding in the company, by Attenborough.

Capital Radio moved into offices in Piccadilly, while the studios underwent construction on the first floor of Euston Tower, opposite Warren Street Underground Station. The building, which is London's tallest office block, was just a stone's throw from the television studios of Thames Television. As soon as they moved into their temporary office, Michael Bukht, the Programme Controller, started interviewing job aspirants. He was once quoted as saying he received 5,200 applications for jobs on the station.

Joan Shenton and Tommy Vance — together they presented the morning show on Capital Radio for nearly a year.

"They've either got the unemployment figures wrong, or a lot of somebodies really want us," he said.

Interviews took place at the rate of one every fifteen minutes, Bukht planned to interview about 200 people for his 40 posts in the presentation department. At the end of each interview he scribbled a summary opinion: "might train into something like a doorman;" "he'd organise me out of my rocking mind;" "she's got a spark — let's fan it."

Capital moved into its new home only a couple of weeks before it was due to go on the air. There were workmen all over the place, cables hanging from ceilings, holes in the floor — organised chaos. According to Dave Symonds, the first deejay to broadcast on Capital Radio, the engineers were still wiring up the control desk hours before his first programme. He literally had only a few minutes to try the studio out before he went on-air!

Sean Day-Lewis, writing in the *Daily Telegraph,* described the opening: "Capital Radio broadcasting for the first time yesterday made a bland and relaxed opening, offering a staple diet of middle of the road pop music decorated with hearts and flowers chat and a direct appeal to the material instincts of listeners."

Programmes started at 5 a.m. with an opening announcement by Chairman Richard Attenborough, followed by the National Anthem in full, with new choral and orchestral "twiddles" by Sir Arthur Bliss; then a Capital jingle. David Symonds hosted the first programme and after saying that Capital was not going to be a station for delivering long diatribes, played Simon and Garfunkel's *Bridge Over Troubled Waters.* He then thanked Richard Attenborough, Brian Forbes and Michael Bukht and others for their existence. "They are the nicest people I have ever been associated with in my entire career." The music was interrupted by news bulletins every hour, and at other times by weather and traffic information. Monty Modlyn was out and about in London talking to people in the streets, although there was some trouble with his portable transmitter.

The second time slot was shared by Tommy Vance and Joan Shenton. Between records they featured a "swop shop," where listeners could ring in and advertise items they wanted to sell or exchange. The first soap opera, *She and Me,* featured a Canadian newly arrived in London chatting to her prospective char. Later

Peggy Mount starred in *The Bedsitter* as Lilly Dawkins, a landlady with a hard exterior, a heart of gold, a soft husband and a restless daughter. Tommy Vance said in his programme that he thought it was the start of something that would become a British institution.

The first transatlantic accent of the day was that of Dave Cash at midday. *Cash's Countdown* was a very simple quiz in which the first contestant knew the answers to the questions — "What is a love seat?" and "when is Hallowe'en?" — and won a refrigerator.

The music format was basically middle of the road. Capital's management had looked at the audience figures of the existing BBC stations in April of 1973. A National Opinion Poll showed that 92 per cent of London adults regularly listened to the radio. Over a period of a week, 52 per cent listened to Radio One, 37 per cent to Radio Two, 31 per cent to Radio Four and 7 per cent to Radio London. Capital wanted to steal its listeners from both the pop music Radio One and the relaxed sweet music Radio Two. It decided on a format, well established on the other side of the Atlantic — a mixture of pop and light music. But Capital Radio was soon dubbed with the name "Radio One and a Quarter" by the press.

Only in the evenings did the format change with a rock show *Your Mother Wouldn't Like It,* hosted by ex-BBC deejay Nicky Horne, then at 8.30 p.m. Alan Hargreaves, a well known Thames Television personality with *Open Line.* It was quite surprising that the IBA allowed both Capital and London Broadcasting to use the same name for their phone-in programmes. *Music, Music, Music* was the title of ninety minutes of specialist music starting at 10 p.m. The week's line-up was as follows: Monday, classical; Tuesday, eithnic; Wednesday, jazz; Thursday, country; and Friday, rock and roll.

Newcasts were presented on the hour, twenty-four hours a day with separate newcasts on the half-hour through the breakfast programme. Under News Editor Ron Onions, a team of eighteen newscasters, producers, editors and reporters compiled the bulletins from information coming from Independent Radio News and from its own local news-gathering sources backed by Local News of London Limited, shareholders in Capital Radio Limited and representing twenty-two newspaper groups in the London area.

During its first fourteen days Capital transmitted over 3,600

Kenny 'n' Cash for breakfast

CAPITAL RADIO
in tune with London

539m Medium Wave – 95·8 VHF Stereo

commercials, an average of 264 a day. During the period over 120 in-house commercials were made. To begin with, the advertising agencies were very sceptical of the success of a Radio 1¼ station, but were prepared to try it. Most of the commercials broadcast were sound tracks of TV advertisements. Only a few advertisers used any imagination. Several newspapers bought spots to advertise what was in today's papers.

But the first audience figures for Capital were disappointing. From a potential audience of over 8½ million, Capital was only just attracting a million. Radical programme and music format changes took place at Christmas 1974. Most of the mini drama serials, *She and Me, The Bedsitter, A King and His Mistress* and radio's first (and last!) strip cartoon *Hazel Adair* were abandoned. To boost the morning shows audience Dave Cash and Kenny Everett, who had been presenting a weekend show, were teamed together. During the 1960's they had presented the *Kenny and Cash Show* on the pirate Radio London. In 1966 it was voted the most popular radio show. *Kenny and Cash* now returned to Capital Radio. The evening specialist music shows were dropped in favour of a music and talk show featuring Sarah Ward and Marsha Hunt.

"We are still experimenting," said Bukht, the Programme Controller. "Our playlist got too big. We were probably not concentrating enough on the audience's tastes as opposed to our own. The sound became more diffuse and the station sounded less coherent."

The station's playlist now consisted of less than a hundred records — at one time it had reached 160 — and reflected the top end of the national pop music charts. One writer said that Capital's new sound made it sound less middle-aged. Head of Music at Capital Radio, Aiden Day, did not necessarily include all chart records in his playlist. He courageously refused to play Lena Zavaroni's *Ma, He's Making Eyes At Me,* in spite of the fact it almost went to number one in the national charts. Her promoter, Hughie Green, sent a cable to Richard Attenborough, protesting at the decision and claimed that Capital's playlist was too American based.

On the other side, Capital played records that were not in the charts. For four weeks, *This Town Ain't Big Enough For Both Of Us* by Sparks was pushed by Capital, until it broke into the charts and Radio One was forced to take it up themselves. The same applied to Cockney Rebel's *Judy Teen,* which received scant attention from the BBC. It went on to become a huge hit, after Capital had stayed with it.

But around late summer 1974, Capital started to shift back again. The music became sweeter and more low-key. The shift reflected a sudden panic, prompted partly by a slump in advertising and that the station was not being adopted by housewives and the older half of its potential audience.

The 15 minute drama series had all disappeared by the summer of 1974, the last to go being *Daple Downs* — a bit like *The Archers* and *Mrs. Dale's Diary*. The Head of Drama resigned as there was nothing for him to do. He was not replaced. The programme structure was simplified and there were rumours that Capital was having financial problems.

In November, the news broke that Capital's running costs were higher than that originally envisaged. To save money it proposed to drop all news and current affairs programmes and make a fifth of the staff of 130 redundant. The newsroom would be completely closed down.

The news of the disbanding of the newsroom came as a shock to journalists on the staff. They immediately rejected the proposals and called on the management to give them full details of the company's financial position. This the management agreed to do and a meeting was arranged for the following day.

When Capital started it had budgeted £200,000 a year for news services. This figure included £98,000 a year to London Broadcasting, for its Independent Radio News service, and the balance for its own news staff. So if the newsroom was to close, and the IRN news bulletins were simply relayed on the hour, it would mean a saving of as least £100,000.

John Witney, Managing Director, would not say how much the station was losing. It was estimated that the running costs were in the region of £175,000 a month. Even in a good month with plenty of airtime sold, there was scarcely enough revenue to cover that figure. Furthermore, the IBA increased the rental for the second year to around £380,000, as it had added a 9 per cent cost of living increase on the previous year.

A few days later Capital Radio went off the air for the first time in its thirteen months life, because of an industrial dispute. Members of the ACTT shop (office branch) stated that they would not accept any redundancies and would not transmit programmes between 1 a.m. and 5 a.m. unless a live presenter was re-instated. The *Night Flight* programme was normally presented by Sean Kelly who was on holiday. No-one had taken his place so a programme went out consisting just of taped music, jingles and commercials. The Engineers' Union won and a presenter was re-instated, after four days.

Negotiations continued between the NUJ and the management over the closure of the newsroom. Eventually agreement was reached over redundancy pay, the newsroom was closed. Since then Capital Radio has simply relayed the first three minutes of the hourly 7-minute IRN bulletin which is also broadcast by LBC and fed by landline to the rest of the ILR network.

In February 1975, Standard Broadcasting Corporation (UK) a Canadian-owned company increased its shareholding in Capital. In a deal which increased the company's issued capital from £650,000 to a million pounds, Standard acquired the largest shareholding, 24.9 per cent. Another Canadian company, Selkirk Communications, had only just increased its holding in LBC to 49 per cent, after the news station had had to raise additional finance, to cover unforeseen costs in its first year of operation. It was an interesting move as it meant that Canadian companies now held the largest shareholdings in London's two commercial stations, yet the IBA had promised in 1972 that foreign interests would not be allowed significant holdings in local commercial radio.

Nicky Horne — presenter of Capital's only rock show.

At the end of its second year, Capital Radio was unable to show a profit, but increased audience figures. The last survey gave the station a weekly cumulative audience of 3,074,000 which made it the world's largest *local* radio station. The programme structure had become more simplified and stable and running costs appear to be kept to the minimum. The future for Capital Radio is still uncertain, but the management and staff are still full of enthusiasm which is probably the most important ingredient for success.

RADIO CLYDE.

Serving West and Central Scotland from transmitters in Glasgow.

First transmission: 31st December 1973.

Estimated Population Coverage: 1,950,000.

Britain's third commercial radio station launched itself in style on New Year's Eve, 1973. Glasgow's Radio Clyde set out from the very first day to be a truly local station. In its application for the franchise, the Company pointed out that all Glaswegians think of Glasgow as the centre of the world. Until the start of Radio Clyde, no other broadcasting medium had looked at the world through Glasgow eyes nor at the area in the sort of detail those who lived there thought it had deserved. Although on the day after Clydeside got its own station, BBC Radio Four's regional service changed its name to Radio Scotland, but still remained very "English." Local radio was desparately needed in the area.

In the summer of 1974, Clyde's Managing Director, Jimmy Gordon, wrote:

"The West of Scotland is the most under-rated area in Britain. Even Glaswegians, though fiercely proud of their City, are often unaware of the assets of our area which justify their pride. Glasgow is not only the football capital of Europe, the scene of tragic fires and the setting of the UCS saga, it has two universities, two airports, Scottish opera, Scottish National Orchestra, beautiful surrounding countryside, the best parks of any British city, the Burrell Collection, the best and hardest pressed social services in Britain, and the birthplace of many famous men. We see it as our job at Radio Clyde to help people in our area to feel justly proud of their many fine achievements and by our success to draw the attention of the rest of the country to the West, which so many commentators are tempted to write off."

Radio Clyde was an instant success with the people of Glasgow. Within a few months it was regarded as the most successful independent station on the air. Audience research showed that more people listened to Radio Clyde than any other station in its coverage area, including Radio One. More than half the population listened to Radio Clyde at some point each day, and over 70 per cent at some point each week. Clyde's late night programmes (10.30 p.m. to midnight) attracted an audience larger than the four BBC channels put together.

The music format on the station is the responsibility of bearded Andy Parks, Head of Entertainment at Radio Clyde. "During the day we produce 'programming'," explained Andy. "We feature various news inserts and other kinds of features, but the music policy relating to those daytime slots is worked out in some considerable detail with the programme planners. Deejays on the station are encouraged to play their own type of music — what they particularly like. If you choose the right kind of guys, you get the right type of music anyway!"

The result is a very loose format. Programmes begin at 6 a.m.

Dave Marshall, Radio Clyde's morning man on the air. *Ford Photo Service*

with the *Breakfast Show* with Dave Marshall, which is very "middle of the roadish," interspersed with news, weather and traffic information. More pop music is featured in the Steve Jones programme, and at midday the format changes again. Richard Park presents the lunchtime show, which during the summer originates from the Radio Clyde Outside Broadcast. The afternoon shows tend more to the middle of the road format again.

In the evenings Radio Clyde completely changes its face with more specialised programmes. "We thought that in the evening the competition that we would have from television would affect the listening figures," explained Andy Parks. "So we designed these programmes so that people could switch on and off. They were not intended for continuous listening. But the listeners don't switch off, they keep on listening."

The early evening programmes include jazz, country and folk, big bands and pop. Later there's soul, rock, nostalgia and album music presented by different deejays each night. The weekends are very much the same as during the week, although there is more of an emphasis on sport. Radio Clyde's two radio cars cover anything happening in the sports world for a four hour programme, Sportsbag, on Saturday afternoons. Sunday's programming includes the *Clyde Top 50*, and *Radio Clyde Worldwide* — a show that has attracted twice as many local listeners as the BBC's *Family Favourites* at the same time.

One reason for Clyde's success could be because of a tremendous amount of teamwork at all levels in the staff. Nearly all the staff on the station come from Glasgow, and very few have worked for the BBC.

One disc jockey, Steve Jones, has worked for the Beeb. He was once a stand-in for Tony Blackburn on Radio One. He prefers working on Clyde to working at the BBC. "Both systems have advantages and disadvantages," explained Steve. "It is just that at Clyde the advantages outweigh the disadvantages. Everybody here is more friendly. Here we have teamwork. At Radio One the only time two deejays see each other is on a change-over, hence there is no station identity. There's only the individual's personality. Here I know everyone and I do everything! I produce programmes, write scripts, make the coffee and sweep the floor."

Another disc jockey, Richard Park, who previously worked on

pirate Radio Scotland and the BBC's *Radio One Club,* agrees with Steve about Radio Clyde. "I'm a great man for Scotland, I've a high regard for this country as I was born, bred and educated in Scotland," said Richard. "It's a dream come true to work on land-based radio in Scotland. I would have been terribly disappointed if I hadn't got the job after hearing the station and the high calibre of the staff from the directors right the way down to the bottom. All the people here have the same idea about radio, although they have different backgrounds. What is happening on this radio station is like no other station," added Richard. "Because it is in an area where there is a very strong nationalistic feeling. This station is for Scots and Scotland! But you would have to be a Scot to know what I mean."

Andy Parks summed up his views on how the station works. "It is like the people of Glasgow. It punches in the face and then runs and hides. The station runs like the people run."

Whether or not it is because being set in the middle of Glasgow

A cheerful line-up in the Radio Clyde music library as deejays mix with members of the pop group, The Rubettes.

makes it unique, one thing is certain. Radio Clyde has really hit the hearts of the Glaswegians. Even the advertisers are pleased with the station. Radio Clyde is a very good example of community radio and also a very successful commercial enterprise.

BRMB RADIO.
Serving the Midlands from transmitters in Birmingham.
First transmission: 19th February 1974.
Estimated Population Coverage: 1,700,000.

The second independent station outside London to go on the air, was BRMB Radio — with a mixture of music, news, information and phone-ins. For three weeks, before the official start of broadcasts, the team of presenters, mostly from the Midlands, had been "dry-running" the station. But work had really begun on BRMB two years earlier.

The man who started the station was David Pinnell, the Managing Director. Before taking up the BRMB challenge, he ran a successful commercial radio station in Lourenco Marques in Mozambique, for ten years. He was also involved in the start of Manx Radio. From the start Pinnell was determined to recruit only professional men and women for all senior positions. He also wanted people who had a knowledge of the Birmingham and Midlands area. Obviously a person's professional qualifications took precedence but BRMB did manage to find nucleus of people who knew the Midlands and its people well.

The first news editor was Birmingham born Keith Hayes, with ten years of commercial radio experience in Canada. The programme director, John Russel, was previously programme organiser for the British Forces Network in Europe. And the sales director, Reg Davies, was formerly with Thomson Publications and ATV.

BRMB's headquarters are in the Alpha Studios in Aston, near Birmingham's famous Spaghetti Junction. Once used by ATV, the studios had to be completely re-designed to form two "on air" studios and the most modern electronic newsroom in the UK. Because the studios are located on the top floor, the presenters have a panoramic view over the city.

At 6 a.m. on the 10th February, "The Sound Way to Spend Your Day" was officially launched. Guests at the opening included the Lord Mayor of Birmingham, Mrs Marjorie Brown, JP, and Lord Aylestone, Chairman of the IBA. Lord Aylestone in welcoming Britain's fourth station said that the Birmingham area had earned itself the just reputation of "The Workshop of the World."

"BRMB will also be a workshop," he said, "breaking new ground in sound broadcasting and aiming to become a first class station in the Independent Local Radio system."

BRMB Radio stressed that the station's programme ingredients would be built around entertainment, information and participation, and at all times it would aim to be simultaneously popular and relevant to the radio audience living in the target area.

Three weeks after it went on the air, the result of some initial research by National Opinion Polls indicated a very large audience listening to the station. Nearly 50 per cent (650,000 adults age 15 years and over) of the potential audience had listened to BRMB in its VHF transmission area along, whilst on an average day 16 per cent (208,000 adults) listened to the station. A more detailed survey, three weeks later, showed that 572,000 adults had tuned into BRMB, during the last week of March. By July the figure had grown to 670,000.

BRMB, the "first with the news" in Birmingham, was itself in the news at the beginning of June. A "task force" of Irish activitists attempted to take over the Aston studios of the station, during the night. Seven or eight raiders entered the building and attempted to broadcast a protest about the death of hunger strike prisoner, Michael Gaughan. They overpowered a commissionaire and ran up to the fifth floor studios. One member of BRMB's news staff, Ken Richards, was slightly hurt in a scuffle as the raiders attempted to grab the microphone. It happened as deejay George Ferguson was putting out his late night programme. None of the thousands of listeners realised what was happening as George quickly shut down the microphone channel. Police arrived and surrounded the building but the raiders had escaped. Later a Republican political organisation known as *Clann na h'Eireann* claimed responsibility for the attempted take-over. Security has since been tightened up.

During its first year, BRMB's programmes gradually matured and a clear identity became established. Early middle of the road formats were replaced by more pop and top forty. New jingles were also produced to brighten up the station's sound. BRMB now broadcasts from 5 a.m. to 2 a.m. Monday to Friday, 6 a.m. to 2 a.m. on Saturday and 7 a.m. to midnight on Sunday.

BRMB's news team has achieved many firsts, mainly due to its electronic newsroom, acclaimed to be the most well-equipped in Independent Local Radio today. In addition to the hourly news bulletins, the news room produces three news programmes a day; the one-hour *First Edition* at 1 p.m. where listeners can phone in their views to the local councillors, MP's and newsmakers; *News Round-Up* at 6.30 p.m.; and a 15 minute *Evening Report* at ten.

The latest survey carried out by RSGB to the advertising industry's specifications shows that BRMB's audience is continuing to rise. Over three quarters of a million adults now listen every week. A very interesting fact revealed by the survey showed that the average Birmingham housewife listens for up to 30 hours a week — a much higher figure than for any other station.

Adrian Juste doing an outside broadcast for **BRMB Radio from the Birmingham Boat Show in 1975.** *Roger Barlow*

DJ Adrian Juste discovers Brian Savin and Ed Doolan on the Severn Valley Railway whilst other BRMB presenters look on, during one of the station's many outside promotions.

Philip Birch, the man who ran Britain's most successful pirate radio station — Radio London — in the sixties, who is now the managing director of one of the most successful

PICCADILLY RADIO

Serving Greater Manchester and the North West from transmitters in Manchester.

First transmission: 2nd April 1974.

Estimated Population Coverage: 2,240,000.

Piccadilly Radio's on-air sequence started in September 1973 with the leasing of premises in Piccadilly Plaza, a shopping centre in the heart of Manchester. The company was then known simply as Greater Manchester Independent Radio Ltd. The first two appointments were the Managing Director, ex-pirate Radio London boss Philip Birch, and the Chief Engineer, Geoffrey White. His job was to design the studios and order the equipment and, together with the architect, supervise the actual construction of the broadcasting station.

He carefully worked out a timing sequence for the building of the six-studio complex. The completion date would be 1st February 1974, so allowing a two month safety period in the event of any construction delays, as the planned opening date was to be 2nd April. Philip Birch later said that nobody had enough courage to suggest starting on April Fool's Day.

All went according to plan. Sales Director Richard Bliss joined the staff and set to work on the rate card. Colin Waters was appointed Programme Controller and his first task was to plan the programme schedule. Other key people joined the staff at the same time — the news editor, sports editor, presentation manager, research manager, company secretary, head of music and the commercial traffic manager.

"Then it happened," said Philip Birch, "the Three Day Week!"

While radio was exempt from Government restrictions during the crisis, suppliers of technical equipment were affected and that caused heavy delays. "Gradually the two-month safety margin was eroded," he continued. "It began to look as if the station would not be on the air by 2nd April. Each day's delay would cost over £2,000, a lot of money for a new company".

Meanwhile other parts of the operation continued. Bob Snyder, the presentation manager, produced what was probably the largest jingle identification package to date. The package, written and orchestrated by John Cameron of *Touch of Class* music fame, consisted of more than fifty cuts based on a tight format. It had four sections, each with ten to fifteen jingles but with the same basic logo and melody line, tailored specifically to programme content and total sound. Earlier the station had listened to submissions from four leading music companies, but its final decision had been to do it themselves.

In the programming department, Colin Waters sorted through 200 applications for about 20 jobs. As there were no studios yet, auditioning had to be done on a small tape machine in the corner of an office. Around the office windows appeared a 200 feet long poster proclaiming "Piccadilly Radio 261 on your wavelength."

As the 2nd April on-air date approached, more and more hitches started to happen. Firstly, the local authority wasn't sure that it could approve the "Link mast" on the top of the building. Secondly, the Post Office wasn't sure that the cable to the transmitter would be completed in time. Finally, and most important to the new station, the three day week had upset the advertising industry. It was becoming increasingly more difficult to sell advertising time.

"Then the Government went to the country," continued Birch. "The mast on top of the building went up, the three day week came to an end, and the final go-ahead decision was made on the Ides of March."

Things then started to go right. Four days before the air date, the news room was completed and £46,000 of advertising bookings arrived from AIR Services, the London Sales Organisation, during a five day period. Finally in the early hours of 2nd April, most of the staff assembled in the back offices looking white, scared and very worried, ready for the 5 a.m. start. At two minutes to five the Piccadilly Radio theme started and at five a nervous Roger Day went on the air with the first DJ programme.

"Nobody said a word for about fifteen minutes," recalled Birch. "Then suddenly everybody, from a slightly delirous Chairman to the much more composed newly appointed receptionist, knew that it was a hit. By lunchtime the congratulatory phone calls and telegrams were flooding in and the people of Greater Manchester started to hum the Piccadilly Radio Jingles."

After two weeks of broadcasting, Piccadilly Radio was being listened to by 1,205,000 adults in the Manchester area, each week, according to NOP "dipstick" research. Half the available audience were tuning into the new station.

Piccadilly Radio is without doubt a pop station, dedicated to playing Top 40 records for every minute the Musicians Union will allow. It is aimed specifically at the teenage and housewife market. All news and information spots are kept to a maximum length of only a couple of minutes so as not to deter any listeners. And the policy works. Another survey carried out in June 1975 showed that the audience had grown considerably. 52 per cent of the adult population in the marketing area were tuning into 261 metres every week.

At the end of October 1974, Piccadilly Radio went 24 hours. Previously it had closed down at 2 a.m., but research convinced the management there was a large enough potential audience to justify the extension. Disc jockeys Tony Emmerson, Phil Griffin and Phil Wood hosted *Piccadilly Nightbeat* from 11 p.m. till 6 a.m. with music, dedications, telephone calls and news.

In April 1975, amid the publicity of the huge losses being made by London's two independent stations, Piccadilly Radio celebrated its first birthday and announced it had made a profit. Philip Birch estimated, on preliminary figures, the station had made a trading profit of around £10,000. The company had projected a trading loss of around £80,000 in its application to the IBA.

"Of course, we're enormously pleased that we've done £90,000 better than we expected," said Birch. "If we can do this well in a year when we have seen a recession, if not a depression, in the economy, then radio must be a sturdy little infant!"

For the year ahead, he hoped Piccadilly's profits would rise to "well in excess of £100,000." He added: "I think we will make it. We are holding the line on costs at the station. The only cloud is the question of how the country's economy goes."

METRO RADIO.

Serving the North East and the Metropolitan County of Tyne and Wear from transmitters in Newcastle.

First transmission: 15th July 1974.

Estimated Population Coverage: 1,700,000.

Without ceremony, Britain's sixth commercial radio station was launched on a Monday morning. At first it was called Metropolitan Broadcasting, then later Metropolitan Radio. Its General Manager was Bruce Lewis — former ITV producer and newscaster. He promised that his station would be different from any other.

"We have a more ambitious programme schedule," said Lewis. "We're all professional broadcasters here and we are putting out a lot more actual programmes — rather than rolling pop. We'll still be using our full needle time but it will be rather more structured."

Many observers regarded the plans for Metro as too ambitious, and they were later to be proved right.

An article in *Script, the Magazine All About Radio,* written by George Box, summarised Metro's weekly schedule:

"Until 5 p.m. the music is a catholic mix. A mix of pop (Teeny bopper and straight pop), national chart soul, MOR stuff, album cuts, including 'melodic' rock plus occasional country and western, folk and jazz items. The proportioning of the ingredients varies with the time of day . . . The music can't be summed up in a word — or the three initials MOR. The policy is good artists, good music, says Peter Lewis."

The station had no actual programme controller. Geoff Coates was director of programmes and Peter Lewis (son of the General Manager) was director of presentation. Each had responsibility for different aspects of programming.

The board of directors of Metropolitan Broadcasting became uneasy about low audience figures and the lack of interest from local advertisers. In November, after five months on the air, Sir John Hunter, Chairman, announced that the appointment of Bruce Lewis as General Manager had terminated. Then, a few weeks before Christmas, the station radically changed its programmes and its management.

Peter Lewis, Head of Presentation, was moved to the post of Head of Outside Promotion. He had been responsible for the no playlist policy, and privately still felt the idea was a good one.

Geoff Coates took up the post of Programme Controller, with Jeff Brown as his Music Adviser. A new style music policy came into operation on the 2nd December. He described the new sound as "eminently middle of the road," a term he loathed but which described for him a musical flavour "compatible with a choice of the best from current pop and from well-known and well tried pop music." The station's overall sound — something which both Coates and Brown felt did not really exist before — would be a "regional reflection of national taste," with deejays' opinions and personal choices being very much taken into consideration, when playlists were compiled. About this time the name was changed to Metro Radio.

"It is really an over-statement to say we've re-launched the station," said Coates, "we have consolidated our professional skills so that we can provide a better, smoother service around the clock."

Neil Robinson, the new Chief Executive who replaced the ousted Bruce Lewis, put it a different way: "We were producing a lot of writing without grammar and punctuation. Now we are aiming to keep most of the words and to present them better with grammar and punctuation."

Metro Radio's Harry Rowell visiting Alnwick's annual town fair.   *Redheads*

A new jingle package was bought from PAMS — an American jingle production house. The station was the first commercial station in the UK to buy station identifications from abroad. Nearly everyone else had either produced their own or obtained them through one of the few British production houses. "The early jingles were long and laborious," explained Coates. "With PAMS we are able to tighten our punctuation. The package has tremendous impact, is exciting and moves."

In February 1975, a new Director, Terry Bate, joined the board and the Canadian company, Standard Broadcasting, took shares in the station. Metro Radio also increased its capital to £500,000. Staff levels were also allowed to run down to 62 permanent staff. Advertising prospects improved and so did the audience ratings.

By July the station appeared to have recovered from its poor beginnings. The cumulative weekly audience was now 37 per cent of adult listeners in the area — an improvement on the 25 per cent figure from the previous October. Metro Radio was now second to Radio One (63 per cent) but leading Radio 2 (35 per cent), Radio Newcastle (30 per cent), Radio Four (26 per cent), Luxembourg 8 per cent and Radio Three (8 per cent).

The Metro day starts at 6.00 a.m. with the *Bill Steele Breakfast Show* — a fast, pacey programme with news every twenty minutes. That's followed by the *Len Groat Get Together*. The programme was previously called the *Groat Market* because of a well known Newcastle street of the same name. But the title proved too successful. Too many weary visitors turned up at the station's Swalwell Studios on the outskirts of Newcastle complaining that they had searched the Groat Market looking for Metro Radio. So when the programme schedules were adjusted during the summer, it changed to its present name.

At 1 p.m. Harry Rowell, the North East's answer to Monty Modlyn, takes to the airwaves. His programme includes quizzes, horoscopes, humour and music. Then the evening drive show is hosted by Giles Squire. *Bil Phil's Music Explosion,* a mixture of soul and progressive rock, fills the early evening spot and then follow the specialist programmes: Soul, Jazz, Nostalgia, Country, Folk, the Arts, Sport, Westminster, North East, Motoring, and phone-ins.

The Metro Radio deejays from left to right—James Whale, John Coulson, Harry Rowell, Len Groat, Dave Roberts, Mike Taylor, Bill Steele, Dave Gregory and Brian McSharry.

SWANSEA SOUND.

Serving South and West Wales from transmitters in Swansea.

First transmission: 30th September 1974.

Estimated Population Coverage: 320,000.

Of all Britain's nineteen independent local radio stations, Swansea Sound has the most difficult task of all, that of being accepted by its community. Because of its locality it is essential that it is a bi-lingual station, and it has to commit a considerable proportion of its airtime to a foreign language, Welsh.

Swansea Sound's programmes originate from studios at Gowerton, on the outskirts of Swansea town. They are located in a small pre-fabricated building that was designed inside especially for Swansea Sound. One of the reasons why the building is situated outside the town is because the company feels that the location helps them associate with a wider area. Another reason for the siting is that there is a large open area attached to the building allowing room for future expansion.

The studios occupy the ground floor of the building and one of the main features of the studio complex is a large sound-proof room with eight-track recording facilities. The control room houses one of the most modern mixer desks in Wales and a tape machine that formerly belonged to Pete Townsend of The Who.

The area with which Swansea Sound has to identify is very industrious. South Wales is the home of the steel industry, coal mining, shipping, and petro-chemical plants. There are also manufacturers of car components, furniture, toys and a substantial agricultural community. The total population in the area covered by Swansea Sound is 350,000, although 173,000 live in Swansea.

The station has a commitment to provide Welsh programming. A condition of the contract between the station and the Independent Broadcasting Authority, requires Swansea Sound to broadcast 10 per cent of its output in the Welsh language. In actual fact, Swansea Sounds exceeds that figure.

Wyn Thomas is the Head of Welsh programming at the station, explained that it was difficult to work out what percentage of the audience spoke Welsh:

"It changes depending on the area you're in — it is a very high percentage as you go to the west and north west of Swansea, but as you go into Swansea Town itself, it falls very low, and as you go through Port Talbot to Cardiff, it falls even further. It wouldn't be fair to give an overall figure. In some parts of the catchment area it is a completely Welsh-speaking community. In this particular community if we didn't broadcast in both languages, it would be very difficult to get a close contact with the listeners."

In its application to the IBA for the franchise, the company had rejected the idea of rigidly separating Welsh language broadcasts from those in English, especially the idea of a wholly Welsh channel.

"We believe that such a sharp dihotomy of the two languages to be dangerous," said the company, "not least to the future of the Welsh language itself since it would tend to isolate Welsh speakers into a cultural ghetto, would diminish the chance of English-speakers making a natural contact with Welsh and could only be a divisive element in our local society."

Chris Harper in the studios of Swansea Sound. *South Wales Evening Post*

During the week the station broadcasts completely in Welsh for ninety minutes at 7 p.m. every night, and at the weekends there is a Top 40 programme in Welsh. Throughout the day there is a policy of integration with regular news bulletins in Welsh, and a short two minute Welsh lesson daily.

The music output is based on a Top 50 playlist, but very rarely does a Welsh record get into the chart. "This is because the output of the Welsh recording industry is very low," explained a deejay, "and also because the production on the records made is very poor, as there are not any good recording facilities available in Wales."

But the situation is changing. A lot of record companies have heard about Swansea's large 8-track studio, and quite a few recording sessions have taken place there. So it is possible that Swansea Sound could have a considerable effect on the future of the Welsh record industry.

The music and programming policy are definitely popular with the audience who have quickly identified themselves with it. When National Opinion Polls conducted a survey in March 1975, it was found that Swansea Sound was the most popular station amongst its listeners, of all the independent stations in the UK.

More than 69 per cent of the population in the area tuned in during the first week of March. More than 185,000 adults were listening to Swansea Sound. The 69 per cent compared with Radio Clyde — 65 per cent, Radio Forth — 47 per cent, Piccadilly Radio — 39 per cent, BRMB Radio — 33 per cent, Capital Radio — 21 per cent and LBC — 12 per cent.

In June 1975, Swansea Sound decided to put 25,000 shares on offer to the public at £1.60 each. Other stations (Orwell, Kennet and Beacon) had just issued shares but had had disappointing results. But that was not the case with Swansea. The demand was so high that there was not enough shares to go round. Charles Braham, Managing Director of Swansea Sound, said that they had been so successful because the station was well established while other stations put shares on offer before they began broadcasting.

"We had a sound to sell and I think that made all the difference," he said. "In addition, we made a profit for the first time in May, and will go on making profits every month for the foreseeable future."

In the original application for the franchise, the Swansea Sound board had told the IBA that as well as the company's founders, mostly local businessmen, they would also offer shares to others in the South Wales community. The issue of shares was not a money-raising exercise, according to Charles Braham.

"Obviously the money coming in will be useful, and will be used to expand our facilities here, but that was not the primary thought behind the issue."

On the 30th September 1975, Wales' first independent local radio station had more than just a year on air to celebrate. It's currently rated as one of the most successful stations in Europe; a survey showing that seven out of ten people in the transmission area listen to it.

"In what has been the worst economic climate for years, we have come in remarkably well on original budgetting," said Braham. "From a revenue point of view, particularly, things are now looking very good indeed, and our projections for year two show a profit in excess of earlier forecasts. In percentage audience terms, we lead the Independent Radio Network so at the moment, thanks to a brilliant piece of teamwork, we seem to be winning on all counts."

Deejays Doreen Jenkins and Chris Harper signing autographs after a successful outside broadcast. *D. L. Harris*

RADIO HALLAM.

Serving South Yorkshire and the North Midlands from transmitters in Sheffield and Rotherham.

First transmission: 1st October 1974.

Estimated Population Coverage: 660,000.

Radio Hallam began as an incorporated company in May 1973, although a consortium which was just a name started a few years before that. The main business interests involved in that consortium came from the Sheffield Newspaper Group, Trident Television, various local industries and Co-ops. When the franchise for an independent local radio service for Sheffield and Rotherham was advertised, Radio Hallam and one other consortium applied.

In April 1974, the IBA announced the contract had been awarded to Radio Hallam Ltd. Immediately the station set to work, and was to be the fastest radio station "on air" from the time it won the franchise to the actual beginning of transmissions. Its target date was 1st October, which according to Managing Director, Bill MacDonald, was for purely commercial reasons.

"The last three months of the year are very vital, from the point of view of sales," explained Bill MacDonald. "In my opinion every station should start with a really strong advertising activity, otherwise you sound and look like a failure — and that dogs you for years afterwards. Some of the other stations on the air have been affected by it."

Disc jockey Keith Skues was appointed the Programme Director on 14th March. Before Radio Hallam, Keith had had a wealth of broadcasting experience. He made his first task recruiting a team of well-known personalities from national radio and complementing them with a number of respected local broadcasters.

Keith first approached Roger Moffat, Johnny Moran and Bill Crozier, and was surprised when they all accepted his offer of employment. Between the four of them they had over 80 years radio experience and had all worked for the BBC, the British Forces Broadcasting Service and Radio Luxembourg.

"I wanted a personality radio station run by professionals," explained Keith. "I knew that these presenters had individual styles and were not exploited to the best of their abilities on other radio networks."

When he advertised for local broadcasters, he received applications from 700 hopeful disc jockeys. But he only took three, all of whom had worked on BBC Local Radio. Later a Women's Editor and a Features Editor were added to the programming staff.

Radio Hallam today is mainly middle of the road music during the day, but carefully chosen to suit most tastes. From 6.00 a.m. to 6.00 p.m. the music centres around a playlist of 100 records — the Top 40 singles, reflected from local sales, 40 selected albums and 20 New Releases. A new playlist is drawn up every week by Skues. In the evenings "non-format" music is played, with certain programmes, like *Hallam Express* featuring specialist music: soul, jazz, country, progressive music, etc. One very popular programme, produced by Skues himself, is broadcast twice weekly and is entitled *20 Years of Rock and Roll.*

Managing director of Radio Hallam Bill MacDonald.

The music of Radio Hallam is interlaced by a set of jingles, with the theme: "It's nice to have a radio station as a friend." Well-known musical director Ray Martin put together 50 jingles which were produced with popular session musicians and singers.

"I still believe that Radio Hallam has the most commercial set of jingles in the entire ILR network," added Keith Skues.

A month after Radio Hallam commenced broadcasts, National Opinion Polls gave Radio Hallam a 25 per cent daily listening figure compared with BBC Radio Two 26 per cent, Radio One 24 per cent and the BBC local station Radio Sheffield 19 per cent. In the summer of 1975 another audience research survey (this time conducted by RSGB) gave Radio Hallam a weekly listenership of 48 per cent of the population in the survey area. Hallam proudly announced that it was the highest level for any station in England — not the UK, as Swansea Sound in Wales had just announced a slightly larger figure. The survey also showed that the primary audience was the 16-45 age group.

In spite of a large audience, Radio Two still holds the biggest slice of the market in Sheffield. But, as Bill MacDonald quickly

The Three Degrees with Keith Skues on a visit to Radio Hallam.

points out, they are using a transmitter with over 400 times the power of Radio Hallam. He would like to see the IBA increase the power of their transmitters.

"I would like to see Radio Hallam expand its coverage," explained the Managing Director. "We've got a coverage officially linked to Sheffield and Rotherham. I think we should be covering the new Metropolitan county of South Yorkshire which has a definable community with Sheffield at the centre both traditionally and historically."

"We ought to have an independent local radio service covering that area," he continued. "The BBC station does in fact do that, although they call themselves Radio Sheffield."

Bill MacDonald would also like to see the station develop to a point where they run a separate FM and AM programme in the evenings. Radio Hallam has the capacity to do that, and it would mean they could increase the programming output, yet remain as just one station.

Keith Skues believes that there are real advantages in having a strong amount of competition with more than one kind of programme to offer listeners on a local basis. "If Yorkshire is the entertainment centre of the North," added Keith, "then Radio Hallam is, in the same way, the leader in its field."

RADIO CITY.

Serving Merseyside and the North West from transmitters in Liverpool.

First transmission: 21st October 1974.

Estimated Population Coverage: 2,200,000.

Radio City — a diplomatically neutral name for a station beaming not only to Liverpool but out beyond Ormskirk, Warlington, and the farther shores of Dee — made the record books from the start as the first provincial station broadcasting 24 hours a day.

Programmes started at 6 a.m. on 21st October. After years of planning, the station was ready to present its own special sound.

The ultra modern studio complex was ready, the staff assembled and the programmes ready to broadcast. All that remained was for the listeners to tune into 194 metres medium wave. From the moment Radio City went on the air, they could hear music, news and a whole range of other programmes with a strong Merseyside flavour.

Most important was that they were in touch with the friendly sound of Radio City 24 hours a day, seven days a week. Programmes started with Arthur Murphy's breakfast show with local, regional and national news. Radio City then combined pre-selected morning music and topical chat with a regular look at the weather, traffic conditions and what was interesting on the Merseyside scene.

In a special newspaper circulated to the residents of Liverpool, the new station stated:

"We're not just another pop station. With the most modern studios in Europe, we'll provide you with the best in contemporary broadcasting. Our music will run from rock to blues, from folk to classic. Our special shows will have you laughing, humming, dancing or just plain listening for sheer enjoyment."

Programming was the responsibility of Gillian Reynolds — Britain's only female programme controller. She explained in the paper what Radio City would sound like.

Gillian Reynolds — Britain's only lady programme controller.

"Radio at its best is the informed friend at the listener's ear," wrote Gillian. "It informs and entertains, amuses and stimulates. And just as good conversation is a two-way flow, we would always hope to engage the listener in a dialogue of ideas, opinion, information. What are we offering which is so different from anyone else? The first round-the-clock radio service, aimed specifically at a majority audience on Merseyside, that's what!"

Radio City claimed to be equipped to deal with any situation. Peter Duncan, the station's Chief Engineer, said that the three studios were designed to deal with every broadcasting eventuality from recording a full orchestra to the live transmission of a chat show. The total cost of the Radio City studio equipment was over £200,000.

Radio City's advertising rates were also very low. A commercial at peak time cost only £54 a minute. The lowest rate being a spot after midnight in the *Nightowl* programme. A 30 second commercial broadcast twice an hour between 2 a.m. and 6 a.m. every night for a minimum period of one year, could be bought at a rate of 51 pence per commercial!

The first indication of the size of the audience on Merseyside came at the beginning of December. A survey carried out during the first three weeks of Radio City showed that 864,000 people were listening. The station had not planned to issue the NOP survey results, but did so after the BBC had issued figures claiming lower audiences for Radio City. The station's Managing Director, Terry Smith, said, "In his now famous letter to The Times on November 15th, the BBC's Head of Audience Research, Mr B. P. Emmett, admitted that the BBC's method does not include sufficient people in each of the commercial local radio areas to furnish reliable estimates for each of them individually. Yet the BBC persists in publishing figures for each commercial station soon after it goes on the air."

"In every case the figures have greatly reduced the commercial station's audience when compared with independent research," he added. "In the case of Merseyside, all three NOP surveys, we have commissioned suggesting that, apart from getting our audience figures completely wrong, the BBC have underestimated the audiences of Radios 1 and 2 and Merseyside, and grossly exaggerated the audience of Radio 4."

Some members of the 70-strong Radio City team.

In February 1975, thousands of radio listeners heard about an air crash as it happened on Radio City. John Darby had been reporting on Liverpool's traffic from an AA plane. He suddenly broke into the Radio City morning programme to say "We've picked up a *Mayday*. We're going to investigate." The spotter plane alerted air-sea rescue services and Darby gave listeners a minute-by-minute account of the search by lifeboats, ferries and RAF helicopters.

The body of the crashed plane's pilot was later recovered by an RAF helicopter. The pilot had been flying to the Isle of Man. Canadian-born John Darby explained that it was the first time Radio City had tried breakfast-time traffic spotting from a plane, and that the *Mayday* message was picked up as they were coming in to land.

More detailed audience figures became available in March 1975, giving City a weekly audience of 964,100. The figures also showed that City was substantially ahead of Radio 2, Radio 3 and Radio Merseyside, always claimed by the BBC as the most successful local radio station.

The music policy on Radio City is the responsibility of Clive Burrows, who used to produce BBC programmes including Eric Idle's *Radio 5,* John Peel, Alan Freeman, and Stuart Henry. He was appointed as a music producer when the station opened, but in November 1974, was promoted to Head of Music. He is responsible for directing the overall music policy of the station as well as compiling the play list, producing the music sessions and all other music programmes. Instead of following the Top 40 format pioneered by the pirates, City has remained very progressively-minded. Burrows has refused to play recent hits by the Bay City Rollers, Mike Reid, the Glitter Band and Telly Savalas, because he feels that those records will let down the rest of his playlist.

One of Radio City's main prides is its ultra-modern news room where seventeen journalists, including specialists on sport, local government and industry, provide news bulletins on the hour, every hour, 24 hours a day. The centre of the news operation is a huge console on which the Duty Editor can control the three outside broadcast vehicles, monitor all other radio and TV channels and automatically transfer Independent Radio News and reporters' contributions to cartridge.

Radio Forth

194

RADIO FORTH.

Serving East Central Scotland from transmitters in Glasgow.

First transmission: 22nd January 1975.

Estimated Population Coverage: 950,000.

Radio Forth, Edinburgh's independent local radio station, took to the air at the beginning of 1975, the first of the last ten stations all scheduled to begin operations that year.

The task of working out a successful programme formula for the new station was that of Programme Controller Richard Finlay. Every company when it makes an application to the IBA for a licence, has a basic format worked out already. The job of the programme controller is to interpret those plans and put them into practical terms, and then fill in the gaps.

"It wasn't too difficult interpreting Radio Forth's plans as the company had been professionally advised," explained Finlay. "The original proposals were practical and not 'airy fairy' like other companies' ideas."

When he took up his position at Radio Forth, he found that there was something like 500 applications for deejay positions on file. Finlay had to wade through this immense series of files and made up a short list of the people he wanted to see.

"I gave preference, for obvious reasons," he continued "to people that were local. The bulk of the staff that were taken on are local to Central Scotland."

He says that Radio Forth's commitment to the community in programming terms is a total one. The music output has a bias towards local artists, and one of the most popular programmes, *Double Scotch* is dedicated entirely to traditional Scottish music.

"We tend to be more speech orientated than, say, Capital Radio in London," he added. "We have longer news bulletins, and two major news 'wraps' every day — *Forth Report* at 1 p.m. and 5 p.m."

Radio Forth is the only station presenting drama every day. When the station started, it was featuring two serials daily. In the mornings there was a bold, bawdy tale of rumpled petticoats and rifled strongboxes. *Deacon Brodie* was the name of the hero and his eighteenth century exploits are a legend. Married and with two mistresses, a pillar of society by day, but by night . . .! In the evenings Radio Forth served up a late night horror series, based on an adaptation of Bram Stoker's great classic of vampires and blood – *Dracula*. Since then the station has followed it with suspense stories.

Radio Forth's music output is the responsibility of DJ Ian Anderson. The station has a Top 40 playlist based on local sales. A large number of returns is obtained so as to ensure a high degree of accuracy.

"From the very first week we were very aware of the stock buying habits of the different kinds of shops in our area," explained Anderson. "Family stores with record departments tended to buy in new records only after they appeared in the National Top 50 and as a consequence ignored local breakouts and frustrated the movement of new releases. Quite the opposite were the almost specialist shops, usually found in the large towns, which stocked rapidly but tended to ignore specific markets."

The *Forth Top Forty* is broadcast in full every Sunday, between 3 and 5 p.m. It is interesting to note that the Forth Forty is one week ahead of the national chart broadcast by the BBC two hours later. For many records the Top Forty programme is the only one in which they will receive airplay all week. Forth's policy is to drop from the playlist all titles which have reached their highest point and are dropping. Exceptions are only made when new releases drop temporarily due to stock starvation in the local shops.

Ian Anderson, DJ and Head of Music at Radio Forth.

The main control desk at Radio Forth. *Alex 'Tug' Wilson*

Radio Forth's Top 40 is quite a costly and time consuming chart to produce, but Ian Anderson thinks that it is worth it.

"We regard it as our weekly market research into the record buying tastes of the local public," he said. "Without a weekly analysis of what's selling in the area, one cannot really judge what music the local people are really interested in."

PLYMOUTH SOUND.

Serving the West Country from transmitters in Plymouth.

First transmission: 19th May 1975.

Estimated Population Coverage: 280,000.

"Plymouth's commercial radio station will become the most successful in the country." That was the prediction of Programme Controller. David Bassett. Shortly after he was appointed, Bassett was interviewed on Hospital Radio Plymouth. He said, "From the way the other stations are going I think that the success of the station and the size of the market are in inverse ratio."

Plymouth Sound was to be "for Plymothians, with Plymothians, by Plymothians."

The Plymouth Sound presenters. Back row from left to right—Carmela McKenzie, Colin Bower and Louise Churchill. Front row—Ian Calvert with David Bassett at the microphone.

"We hope to make it a running story of life in Plymouth with tales of the entertainment sort, news, information, important things and frivolous things. It will cover the whole spectrum of people's pre-occupations."

Bassett explained briefly what he hoped the station would sound like: in the evenings it would be rock music. The programmes for the morning would be designed to reveal local news, information and traffic problems, whilst women at home were to be the main target for the mid-morning and mid-afternoon sessions. In addition, the station would make a point of giving news of events in localities outside Plymouth, that did not receive much coverage in existing media.

But it was to be nearly a year between when Bassett made his predictions and when the station actually went on the air. The first necessity was to raise the required capital. At the end of July 1974, Plymouth Sound invited the public to buy shares in the company. A few weeks later it announced that it had been successful in raising the required amount — £180,000.

Robert Hussell, the company's Managing Director, said, "I look upon our success as a triumph. We set out to raise a lot of money at a very difficult time and succeeded. Our intention was to see that ownership of the station was as diverse as possible. We are particularly pleased that 80 per cent of these shareholders live within our transmission area."

Work immediately started on the studios for the new station. The company had acquired a building in Earl's Acre, Alma Road, that was once an organ factory and about ¼ mile from the city centre. An interesting fact was that the first ever experimental wireless transmissions from Plymouth at the turn of the century were made from the same building that was to house Plymouth's own commercial radio station. The inside of the place was to be completely rebuilt to accommodate a production studio, two self-op control rooms and a talks studio.

In January, twenty-five year old Tim Mason joined as Chief Engineer, after leaving BRMB Radio. At the Birmingham ILR station Tim had been responsible for the design of the electronic newsroom — generally acknowledged throughout the network to be one of the most up-to-date and efficient newsrooms in Europe.

Work on the studios and the recruitment of the 23 full-time staff progressed on schedule. At 6.00 a.m. on a Monday morning in May, Plymouth Sound was heard for the first time. The first voice was not one of the programming staff but a genuine Plymothian. Nine year old Andrew Knight's name had been picked out of a hat by David Bassett. He made the opening announcement, and then for the rest of the day was treated like a celebrity.

Andrew's opening was followed by a record then Colin Bower, presenter of *Sunrise Sound*, a four hour show including music, time checks, road reports and the *Plymouth Journal*.

Sunrise Sound was followed by *Phone Forum* with David Bassett in the chair. Plymouth Sound claimed the programme was a vehicle for spontaneous comments on events of the moment.

Midday programmes included one mainly for women and the last four hours to closedown at 10 p.m. was taken up by the *Ian Calvert Show* — the only pop/rock show on the station. On the opening day Ian Calvert featured an interview with the pop group, Slade.

On Saturdays the tempo changed to include sports coverage as well as music and magazine topics and also an *Armed Forces Hour*. Folk and jazz music with a share of "religious non-religion" programmes filled the Sunday spots.

Plymouth Sound is very different to other stations. Because of the demographics of the audience pattern, very little pop music is played. Plymouth, in the eyes of Managing Director Bob Hussell, is the home of the wife of the Chief Petty Officer, so the station has to cater accordingly. Consequently the music emphasis is more on light music with a dash of country, variety and middle of the road.

The first audience survey was carried out ten days after the station opened by a team from Plymouth Polytechnic. The results indicated that 180,000 people (or 66 per cent) had tuned in at some time in the opening days. However, more detailed research and to the specifications of the advertising industries, was planned for late 1975. One will have to await the results of that before any accurate figures can be obtained.

In October 1975, Plymouth Sound was given permission by the IBA to extend its broadcast hours. It now closes down at midnight instead of 10 p.m. On announcing the extension, Robert Hussell said that he thought it was a marvellous achievement that the smallest commercial station then on the air could extend itself, after just six months operations.

David Bassett with Andrew Knight opening Plymouth Sound at 6 a.m. on 19th May 1975. *Robert Chapman*

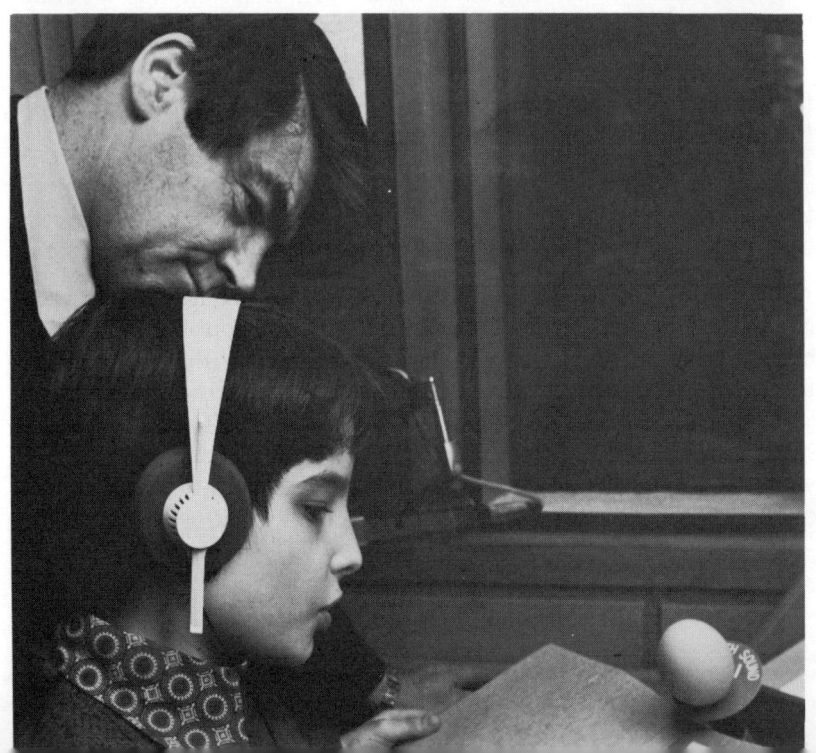

TEES 257

RADIO TEES.
Serving Cleveland County, South Durham and North Yorkshire from transmitters on Teeside.
First transmission: 24th June 1975.
Estimated Population Coverage: 680,000.

On the closing date for applications for the Teeside radio franchise, the IBA was probably horrified when it realised it had only received one application. Only one company, Sound Broadcasting (Teeside) Ltd., had entered the contest. Teeside was the first area that had produced only one applicant, but the contract would not necessarily be awarded by default. "The application will be considered in just as much detail as the applications for other areas," said the IBA, "and if the group concerned does not meet the necessary standard, it will not get the contract."

The IBA would not say what would happen if this group was not allocated the contract. Teeside might have to go without a commercial station, or applications might have to be invited again. Nor would the IBA venture an opinion on why there should be so few people interested in running the station. One theory was that several groups interested in the contract might have banded together to make sure of getting it, although this could not be substantiated.

After several months of deliberations, the Authority announced that it would award the contract to Sound Broadcasting (Teeside) Ltd.

Early in 1975, the company's board decided the on-air name of the station would be Radio Tees. John Bradford, Managing Director of the station, explained why the station was given that name:

"We struggled to find a factor that unified the area lying to the North and South of the River Tees. Without doubt the Tees has been a physical barrier in the past and there is nothing like an old family estate or history across this river. We therefore thought that it was the one unifying force to this area. Itself, it has been a source of entertainment and employment for many hundreds of years. Perhaps this is what a radio station should now set out to do."

Radio Tees moved into a red brick Victorian-style building,

formerly occupied by the Water Board, in Dovecot Street, Stockton-on-Tees. John Bradford described the location as "A central urban site." Chief Engineer Chas Kennedy was brought in to supervise the building and installation of the studios. One unique feature of the studios which are located on the ground floor, is a double-glazed picture window between the major on-air studio and the reception area. As you enter the building you immediately see the deejay on-the-air.

Shortly before Radio Tees' on-air date of the 24th June, 1975, Bradford described the new station: "It's friendly radio . . . it's vital radio . . . above all it's local radio."

From six in the morning to twelve at night, Radio Tees entertains and informs its potential audience of 680,000. The morning shows are designed to brighten breakfasts, melt traffic jams and ease tedious household chores. In the afternoons there's more music and discussion to please the housewife, and then later to help their husbands through the long drive home. From 7.30 p.m. to 9 p.m. there are various shows depending on the day, ranging from folk and rock to the Top 40. The last three hours of the day go to Tees' lovely lady of the night, Tricia Ruff, with the *Late On* programme, a relaxed gentle show with records, interviews and occasional live spots from the local night scene.

Radio Tees is a music based station, but it reflects a broad, popular spectrum of interests. News is broadcast every hour on the hour. The news operation is in the hands of Bill Hamilton, who's had broadcasting experience with Tyne Tees Television, BBC Radio and BBC *Nationwide* in Scotland. He has six reporters working under him to cover all local news stories. National and international news is taken from the hourly three minute Independent Radio News feed.

"Our motto is 'Your friendly local radio station'," said John Bradford, "and we mean just that."

RADIO TRENT.

Serving the City of Nottingham from transmitters in Nottingham.

First transmission: 3rd July 1975.

Estimated Population Coverage: 600,000.

The franchise for the Nottingham independent local radio service was awarded by the Independent Broadcasting Authority to the Radio Trent consortium in July 1974. It was headed by Norman Ashton, a solicitor with local industry ties. With him there was another thirteen directors, many with strong theatrical ties. The largely amateur Robin Hood theatre at Aversham near Newark supplied two, Mrs. Valerie Baker and Miss Marjorie Lyon. Jack Barham was a director of Moss Empires which owned the Theatre Royal in Nottingham; and among those connected with the Nottingham Playhouse were a Conservative Councillor, Bernard Bateman, and a veteran Labour Councillor, Charles Butler. Freelance journalist Ailsa Stanley was also a director of the Playhouse Trust.

Other directors included Denis Maitland, a former executive with pirate Radio London and later Radio Luxembourg, and Terrence Kelly, a freelance broadcaster. Maitland was appointed Managing Director and immediately set about getting Radio Trent on the air.

In the spring of 1975, the company moved into a building in Castlegate, a shopping centre in the heart of Nottingham. It was a

The Radio Trent team—Back row from left to right—Peter Quinn, John Peters, Guy Morris, Chris Baird, Kid Jensen, Graham Knight. Front row—Jeff Cooper and Bob Snyder (Programme Director).

Kid Jensen in the Radio Trent studio. *Marshalls*

Regency building with four floors, and a basement underneath. It had once been used as a women's hospital and the basement had been the morgue which Radio Trent's studios were now to occupy.

Bob Snyder, ex-pirate deejay, moved from Manchester's Piccadilly Radio — where he had been Presentation Manager — to take up the post of Programme Controller. Shortly after his appointment, he was asked what the station would sound like.

"It's very early," he said, "as we don't come on the air until June, to lay down any rules about the programming. But generally during the day it will be broadly music. In the evenings it will broaden out a bit, probably towards rock."

He promised that Radio Trent would have a completely different sound to any other station. He decided that his on-air team of presenters would be a balance of professional broadcasters and the local element.

"I'd like to bring in a mixture of local people," continued Bob Snyder, "and people from outside the area. I think outsiders will stimulate the locals, who will contribute the local knowledge. I think that we will be able to do that very well."

A few months later he announced the deejay appointments.

Only one well-known name, Kid Jensen, was included in the line-up of nine. Canadian Jensen had spent six years with Radio Luxembourg, and before that had had experience in Canadian commercial radio. Three others, John Peters, Chris Baird and Peter Quinn, came from UBN — the industrial radio network — where Snyder himself had once worked. Graham Knight and Peter Wagstaff were both local to Nottingham and only had experience of hospital broadcasting stations. One member of the team recruited by Snyder, Guy Morris, had never worked on a radio station before in his life — not even a hospital radio station.

"I get into depressing conversations with people about how to get into radio," Bob explained. "The answer is that you need experience, but how do you get experience when you can't get a job? Guy is a practical demonstration of how you can do it. Apart from basic lack of writing in at the right time, he demonstrated that he could do it, through a series of tapes which were excellent!"

On 3rd July 1975, the station commenced broadcasts and immediately one of the features that made Radio Trent different from the others became obvious. Radio Trent broadcasts "programming," not "programmes." The deejays don't say a lot, although there is clear station identity. Across the day there is a shift in emphasis in the music format.

"From 6 a.m. — 5.30 p.m. we broadcast a flow of broadly based contemporary popular music," explained the programme director. "The music policy is very broad, but we tend not to play re-releases and we tend not to play novelty records. Basically it's from mainstream pop over and towards contemporary sounds. We play 40 oldies a day, mainly during the peak housewife listening times."

From six to midnight, the station moves a lot closer to contemporary music and progressive rock, and aims the programmes at the student audience. Within the catchment area of Radio Trent are three Universities — Nottingham, Leicester and Loughborough, resulting in a high student population. The music format is mainly based on album tracks but also features a lot of experimental material.

Snyder has plans of doing the occasional weekend special — like 48 hours of just the Beatles. Generally the format at the weekends is much the same as during the week, but with more emphasis on sport, and slightly more relaxed.

Radio Trent takes advantage of the fact that Radio One has a very poor signal in the area, so goes for the pop audience rather than be a Radio 1½, trying to steal listeners from the two national networks. The station is hoping to become as acceptable to its own community as a local newspaper. There are some parts of the reception area where every household takes a local paper. Radio Trent would like to see itself reach that kind of acceptance, where everybody listens to the local station. They think that Radio Trent's programming policy will make it the "most-listened-to" independent station. Bob Snyder says that there is one important reason why Trent will be the most successful ILR station: "Nottingham is a superb place to run a radio station!"

PENNINE RADIO.

235 Pennine Radio

Serving West Yorkshire from transmitters in Bradford.

First transmission: 16th September 1975.

Estimated Population Coverage: 40,000.

The idea behind the company that started Pennine Radio was the brainchild of Steven Harris, the station's deputy news editor. In 1972 when it was first announced that there might be a commercial radio station in Bradford, Steve was a journalist with the *Bradford Telegraph and Argus*. He contacted several fellow journalists and a handful of local councillors who showed interest and a committee for Radio Bradford was formed.

At that time it was half expected that British commercial radio would follow the American pattern of endless pop music, but the committee held the belief that whatever its form of control, local radio was primarily a public service, reflecting community life. People of course had to be persuaded to listen to it so the new station would have to play records.

"But it must be more than musical wallpaper," said Harris. "What counts are the items between the records. The programmes must be informative and enthusiastic yet at the same time entertaining and every effort should be made to involve the people which the station serves."

Harris and his Committee approached local businessmen and broadcasters, inviting them to join the Committee. He soon found that all his spare time was being spent on typing out minutes and circularising members. At the same a rival group, Aire Radio, founded by Bradford businessmen and Peter Harland, a former editor of the *Bradford Telegraph and Argus,* was preparing the plans.

"Then came our break," said Harris continuing the story, "I was up at the University talking to Lester Hall, President of the Students' Union, when he mentioned that a certain Stephen Whitehead, business manager of *Time Out,* the London entertainment magazine, had popped in, seeking opportunities to start a local magazine."

Steven Harris arranged to meet up with Stephen Whitehead and told him of his plans for local community radio. He was immediately interested and agreed to take up the job of full time organiser. He was also prepared to put his life savings of £300 into the company, from which he would pay his own wages for three to four months. Among those who joined the group was TV personality Austin Mitchell, who was later to become Pennine's Programme Advisor.

The first substantial donation to the funds came from the National Union of Dryers and Bleachers. A charitable body representing about 200 local organisations, called the Bradford Community Radio Trust, was next set up. The Trust has a financial stake, so when profits begin to flow in a couple of years' time, the Trust's share will be used for charitable work in Bradford.

Stevie Merrike of Pennine Radio.

After a two-cornered fight for the franchise, Bradford Community Radio Ltd. was awarded the contract. Many people were surprised that the IBA had favoured the smaller group, against the Aire Radio consortium which had the backing of Bradford Corporation.

"For the people who put money into Bradford Community Radio, it was a gamble," added Harris, "but no-one stood to lose too much if we failed. We had adopted an attitude of healthy pessimism. We haven't aimed at lofty schemes and all our plans have been down to earth and financially sensible.

Bradford Community Radio had proved that a small almost penniless group with sufficient enthusiasm could beat the odds. Not that it lacked money now it had the franchise.

In March 1975, it was decided that the station would be known as Pennine Radio on the air. "We believe that is is important that the radio station serving the whole of the Bradford Metropolitan District and beyond, has an identity that everyone in the station's reception area can associate with," explained Stephen Whitehead, now the Managing Director. "Our research has shown that despite local government re-organisation, local loyalties are still very strong. Indeed, the coincidence of local government re-organisation and steep rises in the rates seems to have increased local chauvinism in some of the former Urban Districts. We have chosen a name therefore that has a local connotation throughout our broadcasting area.

"In any case," continued Whitehead, "as our studios will be in Pennine House, Forster Square, being called Pennine Radio will make it that bit easier for people to find us."

At 6 a.m. on 16th September 1975, Pennine Radio, Britain's fourteenth independent local radio station, was officially launched. A £10,000 launch promotion had preceded the first week's transmissions and included advertising on television, in newspapers, on posters and buses.

Pennine's weekday programmes start with a three hour breakfast show presented by deejay Stevie Merrike. Merrike is the station's deputy Programme Controller and his responsibilities include the supervision of the deejays and the music policy. The breakfast show is followed by *The Morning Programme* with former LBC presenter, Stewart Francis. Every day at 12.30 there's a fifteen minute newsbreak presented by Tony Cartledge and Stephen Harris. Afternoon programmes are presented by Roger Kirk (12.45 − 4 p.m.) and Julius K. Scragg (4 − 7 p.m.). Later in the evenings there is a one-hour phone-in and a 15 minute *Asian Magazine* programme. Specialist music is broadcast from 8.45 to 10 p.m. and then Liz Allen takes Pennine through to closedown at one.

RADIO VICTORY.

Serving Greater Portsmouth and part of the Isle of Wight and the Solent from transmitters in Portsmouth.

First transmission: 14th October 1975.

Estimated Population Coverage: 460,000.

The name of the company that won the Portsmouth ILR franchise was Sound Broadcasting (Portsmouth) Limited but shortly afterwards the name was changed to that of one of its competitors that had been absorbed into the consortium. Programmes of Radio Victory began on the 14th October 1975 at 1 p.m. with Glen Richards saying, "For the very first time in the South of England with the time just gone one o'clock . . . this is Radio Victory. My name is Glen Richards and, together with almost ninety other people, some of which you will never hear and to whom I now pay tribute for their hard work and time, and above all their love that has brought you your station, I begin as we all shall continue, to try and bring you everything that touches you."

During the celebrations that followed Managing Director Guy Paine was asked what he thought Radio Victory could do for Portsmouth. He replied that he hoped that it could give Portsmouth a greater sense of community feeling. "One of the great disappointments to the staff who had moved to Portsmouth was to find that there wasn't a great community spirit within the city," he explained. "Areas of the city tend to be contained within themselves."

The only thing that marred the opening of the station was a small demonstration by a group of Portsmothians protesting on Victory's doorstep about the fact that so few of the station's staff were from Portsmouth, and that it did not represent the community as such. Victory replied that all its staff would soon be residents of the city, when they had found suitable accommodation.

Dave Symonds was the first disc jockey to present a programme on Capital Radio when it started in October 1973. Now he is the Head of Programmes at Radio Victory in Portsmouth.

Programming at Radio Victory is the responsibility of former deejay Dave Symonds who prefers the title of Head of Programmes. Most stations decide their programme format then go out to find the deejays to fill it. Symonds, who has worked for the New Zealand Broadcasting Corporation, the BBC, Radio Luxembourg and Capital Radio, had a different procedure. Instead he first recruited a first class team of presenters and deejays then held a meeting between all of them to discuss what the programme format should be like. Symonds picked a balanced team of professionals and new people. "That way the new blood pick up techniques from the pros, and the ageing rockers like me can lose a few years and a few pounds by gaining some of the enthusiasm of the newcomers," he said. To see that the programme format stays on the right lines, Radio Victory intends to hold a public meeting once every three or four months — it had two before it even went on the air — at which listeners will be invited to attend and state their views on the station and its output. "We have set up a volunteer listeners' forum," added Symonds, "because the most important thing about Radio Victory is that it is open to criticism."

RADIO ORWELL.

Serving Suffolk and part of Essex from transmitters in Ipswich.

First transmission: 28th October 1975.

Estimated Population Coverage: 210,000.

Of all the independent local radio stations, Radio Orwell will serve the smallest area. The man who started the company was Commander John Jacob, a farmer and director of several companies with agricultural interests. When the IBA announced that Radio Orwell had won the franchise, Commander Jacob was asked by a local reporter if he stood by a remark he had made in 1972, that local radio should be "fun".

"I think they have to be interesting, amusing and entertaining, although I do not mean trivial", he replied. "I feel they have to take a prominent role in the life of society and that does mean being fun, in the broadest sense of the word."

Several months after being awarded the franchise, Radio Orwell made a public offer of shares in the company. In its prospectus the company forecast a net income of £144,000 in the first year, but because of the high cost of setting up the station a net loss of £29,000 was expected. But in the second year, a profit of £9,500 was anticipated with a net income of £215,000 rising to £310,000 in the following year resulting in a profit of £65,000. The share issue of £229,332 was a success and Donald Brooks, Managing Director said he was very relieved in view of what had happened when the Reading and Wolverhampton stations went public.

Radio Orwell moved into its new headquarters soon after at Electric House in Lloyds Avenue, Ipswich. While the studios were being constructed in the basement of the former Eastern Electricity Board building, an old tunnel was uncovered. No-one at Radio Orwell knows where the tunnel leads as it was blocked off by the building contractors shortly after it was discovered. Only the opening remains, which the station uses for storage of the several hundred audition tapes that it has received. One member of the staff remarked at the time that Radio Orwell could become the first haunted independent radio station!

The station's programme output is the responsibility of Australian John Wellington. At the age of 30, he had had fourteen years of radio experience, mostly down under. When he arrived in England in 1973 he joined Capital Radio and worked in a variety of jobs, then a year later joined Metro Radio as commercial production manager. At Radio Orwell, his first job was to recruit a team of four presenters. He chose three ex-pirates Andy Archer, Greg Bance and Keith Rogers and a Metro Radio man Harry Rowell. Musically, the station is very middle-of-the-road but varies across the day from pop to progressive music. Because the station only has a small staff, programmes end at 8 p.m. after an hour-long phone-in programme, although Radio Orwell then stays on the air for a further two hours playing continuous music.

DOWNTOWN RADIO.

Serving Belfast and Northern Ireland from transmitters in Belfast.

First transmission: Early 1976.

Estimated Population Coverage: 975,000.

The company which was awarded the Belfast franchise by the Independent Broadcasting Authority early in 1975 was known as Community Radio Services Limited, but like so many of the other independent radio contractors it wanted a better name for use on the air. In August 1975, David Hannon, the chief executive, announced that the radio station was looking for a new name. "We've got to get a name which not only avoids confusion with the BBC's Radio Ulster (the regional Radio 4 service) but must be acceptable to all sections of a fragmented and very sensitive community," explained Hannon. "We've had over 500 suggestions so far. Everything from Radio Rainbow to Radio Atlantic and most of the geographical names such as Radio Belfast and Radio Ards — the studios we are building are at Kiltona just outside Belfast on the Ards Peninsular."

The company eventually decided on the name Downtown Radio, partly because it is located in County Down, and because they did not want to over-identify with the area geographically. David Hannon, the managing director, is himself an Ulsterman. He worked for the BBC in Northern Ireland between 1960 and 1970, then became the Director-General of the Malawi Broadcasting Corporation for two years. He then returned to this country and the post of station manager at BBC Radio Leicester, until he joined the new Belfast station.

According to Hannon, the station will probably be mostly middle of the road. A survey carried out by the company showed that Northern Irelanders are hungry and thirsty for Country and Western. "C & W came streets ahead of any other type of music," said Hannon, "so Downtown's programme planners will be bearing that in mind."

"Because of the Northern Ireland situation," he continued, "keeping people up to date with what is happening is more important in this area than it is for any other station. We must have a very efficient news operation."

Downtown Radio is expecting to start broadcasting early in 1976. The IBA will not allow the station to announce an exact date until it is certain that everything is in order, but many of the Irishman involved in the station will be bitterly disappointed if Downtown Radio is not on the air by St Patrick's Day.

BEACON RADIO.

beacon radio303
for the West Midlands

Serving the Black Country and West Midlands from transmitters in Wolverhampton.

First transmission: March 1976.

Estimated Population Coverage: 1,240,000.

A similar situation to the Teeside incident occurred when the Independent Broadcasting Authority advertised for applicants for the independent local radio franchise for Wolverhampton. Only one applicant, Beacon Broadcasting Limited owned by the local paper the *Express and Star,* applied for the franchise. The Authority was anxious that there should be a local station in Wolverhampton, so they awarded the contract to Beacon, although they had reservations about its ownership and financial structure. One of the first moves of the newly appointed company was to recruit a chief executive. Jay Oliver, an American who had spent most of his working life in radio, television, newspaper advertising and promotion, took up the post. He came from Belfast Telegraph Newspapers where he had been Sales Promotion Manager and was responsible for that company's interests in commercial radio in Northern Ireland. From early 1974 he was seconded from the Belfast Telegraph, to form the successful Community Radio Services Ltd. application for the Belfast ILR franchise.

Beacon Radio's programme controller, Allen MacKenzie said, "I'll start as I intend to continue — you know how thrifty we Scots are!"

An attempt to raise capital for the station, by going public, failed early in the summer of 1975. The share issue of 349,000 £1 ordinary shares was under-subscribed so on the 23rd May, Jay Oliver announced that the company would go private. The station was to go ahead but on more modest lines than had originally been planned. The budget for premises and equipment was reduced, and it was announced that the company would not be using as headquarters the Burntree House office block just south of Wolverhampton, near Dudley. "It was too deluxe for us," explained Oliver, "We now have our sights on alternative premises". He also revealed that the staff would now be 39 instead of 46 and that Minis would be used instead of Ford Escorts for company use.

Towards the end of the summer, the company found suitable premises for its studios and offices at Tettenhall Road, Wolverhampton. "I feel we have been very lucky in finding such an interesting and suitable building," continued Oliver, "It will provide our staff with unusually pleasant surroundings, which can only be a positive influence on our 'on-air' sound."

At the same time the station found a new name — Beacon Radio 303. The Independent Broadcasting Authority expects to have both the medium wave and VHF stereo transmitters ready by January or February 1976, but Beacon do not anticipate the studio complex and offices to be complete until at least March.

When full transmissions begin there will be a large overlap between its service area and that of neighbouring BRMB Radio in Birmingham. Jay Oliver is confident that Beacon's bright and bold up-tempo format will steal a large number of listeners from BRMB Radio.

THAMES VALLEY BROADCASTING

Serving Reading and part of West London from transmitters in Reading.
First transmission: March 1976
Estimated Population Coverage: 270,000.

When Radio Kennet was awarded the IBA franchise for the area, the *Reading Evening Post* carried the headline "Outsiders Win Radio Reading Battle." Spokesman for Radio Kennet, Ted Ball, assistant registrar at Reading University, said, "We are delighted that we have been given the opportunity to take up the challenge, and we shall do our best to make the station truly representative of Reading." But he warned: "In these difficult times we hope people will not expect too much from us at first."

Mr Ball went on to say that in a few weeks time the company would be making an issue of shares, to which the public should be invited to subscribe. "Special preference will be given to people in Reading, " he added.

On the 29th April, Radio Kennet advertised the issue of 350,000 shares at £1 each. The minimum holding was to be £50. But the issue was not successful. As the shares were advertised, director Sir John Colville said: "It's up to the people of Reading to make sure we get this station off the ground. If we do not raise the necessary amount of equity the idea will fall flat on its feet and Reading will never have its own radio station!"

Neil ffrench-Blake, the Chief Executive, revealed only a week before the closing date that the share issue was not fully subscribed. "Everybody knows my ambition is to run the only station in the country owned by the audience," he said. "It will be a great disappointment if I fail. But I will not sacrifice the station for the sake of this ideal. If necessary we will get the money from Japan — and this is not impossible the way things are going."

A week later it was revealed that only 200 local investors had applied for shares. The exact amount was not disclosed, but it was stated that all the money would be returned as the share issue had been under-subscribed. The closing date was 28th May 1975. Neil ffrench-Blake blamed the referendum on the Common Market (5th June) for the company's failure to persuade the city to come up with the cash. Financiers were awaiting the outcome before making investments.

The company was put into "mothballs", and hopes of being on the air by Christmas 1975 faded. Then several months later it was announced that Radio Kennet would be run as a private company but with new backers. At the end of October 1975, Neil ffrench-Blake made a further announcement. The board of directors had decided that the name of the company would be changed to Thames Valley Broadcasting, as it was felt that that name gave a better description of the service area. At the same time ffrench-Blake revealed some details about the programmes of Thames Valley Broadcasting. A team of nine broadcasters would front the station in four-hour strip shows for eighteen hours a day. It would have a middle of the road format and there would be a high accent on access programming.

9 Independent Radio News

The following is a reprint of an article by the author about Independent Radio News which appeared in the Radio Guide in January 1975:

COMMUNICATIONS House, in Gough Square near Fleet Street, is just a stone's throw from Dr Samuel Johnson's house. It is the home of LBC – London Broadcasting – the all-news commercial radio station. It is also the home of Independent Radio News (IRN).

Independent Radio News is the sister company of LBC that collects news and distributes it to the independent local radio network. It is located in the basement of Communications House and is probably one of the most modern radio news rooms in the world.

News reports come into IRN from various sources. One of the main news inputs is the teleprinter room. Reports come in by wire from twelve newsprinters. IRN takes three feeds from the Press Association, two from UNS, two from Reuters and one from UPI. There are an additional four teleprinters for sports results.

All the reports from the teleprinter room are taken to a ten-sided control desk. Each position has an electronic switchboard with twenty telephone lines and facilities to monitor the outputs of IRN, LBC, BBC Radio, Television sound or other sources like the radio car or the AA weather centre feeds.

A copy taster at the desk reads every teleprinter report. He passes home news to the Home Editor on his left and foreign news to the Foreign Editor on his right. Around the far side of the desk sits the Sports Editor.

Control Room to the main studio at London Broadcasting. *Martin Stevens*

The Home Editor has two deputy editors and the Foreign Editor has one. News reports are sifted and in each case the Editor decides what stories are to be taken. The Foreign Editor passes his material to the Home Editor who picks a selection of his own home news and the Foreign Editor's news. This he passes to his Chief Writer who sits on his left. He writes the scripts that are eventually read by the news reader.

IRN also takes audio — news feeds. These come from a variety of sources. Two news agencies, Reuters and UPI, have audio services. Most of IRN's reports from correspondents abroad come through these agencies. Notice of the reports due to come through are printed out on a teleprinter. The editor then decides which reports he will use, so when the reports come through, they are recorded in a special control room.

The control room can also take reports from telephone lines where ILR stations and freelances can ring in their reports. They are recorded on to tape and edited if necessary. They are then transferred on to cartridges or "carts."

The editor decides on the balance between reports that are read by the newsreader and those on "carts." The intention is for the news to sound "authoratitive" so IRN tends to only use audio reports which are interviews or reports of something actually happening, i.e. actualities.

IRN has seven full time reporters that can be sent anywhere in the country at any time. They also have about 200 freelance

One of the two news control desks in the newsroom of LBC/IRN.   *Martin Stevens*

"stringers" throughout the UK. IRN can also call on the reporters and facilities of the newsrooms of the ILR stations around the country.

There are direct lines into Communications House from Westminster and the GLC. Very often a special line is set up by the Post Office if an important speech is being made from somewhere. A radio car is available to IRN for broadcasting "music quality" reports to the newsroom. But usually telephone lines are adequate for most reports.

Independent Radio News presents one news bulletin an hour which is broadcast live on LBC. The news on the half-hour is London news and is produced by LBC's own news staff. The hourly bulletin is also fed by wire to the 19 ILR stations around the country.

Each of the commercial stations operating use IRN and their own news rooms. The local news rooms tend to concentrate on local news only. The national and international news is fed to the network stations in two ways.

A teleprinter is constantly sending out IRN's output to the network and continually updating it. Between London and each station there is also an audio feed. Audio reports which are on the "carts" are fed to the local stations at quarter past the hour every hour. Any fresh reports are fed through at half-past and quarter-to-the-hour.

At the other end of the wire, the local news room record the reports. The local station's news editor decides which reports to use and they are then transferred to "carts" and used in the news bulletin.

Some of the local commercial stations re-write the reports they receive on the IRN teleprinter. But most take the reports direct and read them in their own newscast.

Graham Freer reading the IRN bulletin on the hour. *Martin Stevens*

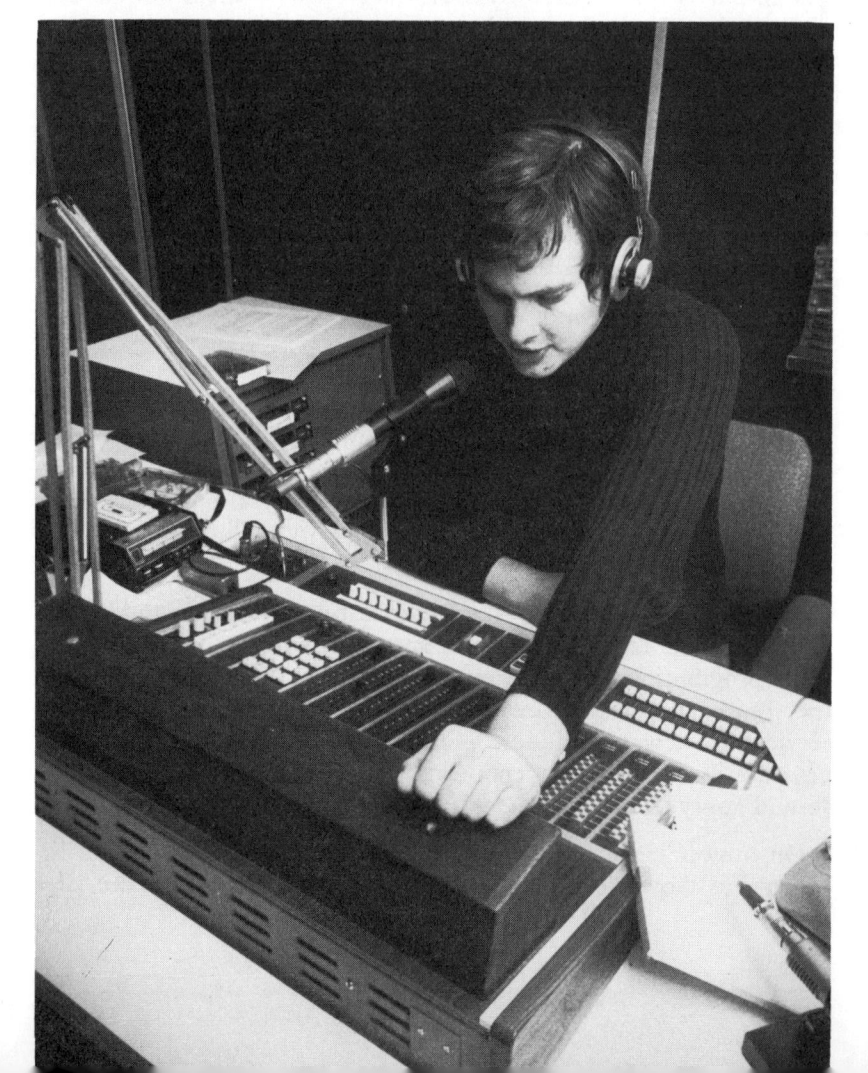

10 Labour Party Halts Expansion

IN SPRING 1973, there was another General Election. At that time the IBA had offered eleven contracts to stations and had just invited applications for the Nottingham and Teeside franchises. The closing date for the last two invitations was a week before the Election. The result was a change of power and the return of the Labour Government.

Immediately the IBA suspended all plans for advertising for further contracts, although it continued the process of finding and acquiring transmitter sites and ordering equipment far ahead. Lord Aylestone, Chairman of the IBA, said he did not know when the Authority would be advertising contracts again. He also said that he was anxious to know the Government's intentions.

One of the first moves of the new administration was to revive its plan to set up a broadcasting committee of inquiry under the chairmanship of Lord Annan, Provost of University College, London. The committee had been shelved by the Conservatives when they took office in 1970. It had the following terms of reference:

"To consider the future of the Broadcasting Services in the United Kingdom, including the dissemination by wire of broadcasts and other programmes and of television for public showing; to consider the implications for present or any recommended additional services of new techniques; and to propose what constitutional, organisational and financial arrangements and what conditions should apply to the conduct of all these services."

On announcing the appointment of the sixth committee in 51 years, the Government extended the BBC Charter and the IBA

Act by three years so that it would expire in July 1979. But no statement was made with regard to commercial radio.

Another early decision made by the Government, was to dissolve the Ministry of Posts and Telecommunications. The sponsorship of the Post Office was transferred to the Secretary of State for Industry and its functions in the field of broadcasting to the Secretary of State for the Home Department. The Home Office are directly responsible for the police, and there was much criticism of the move which could be the first step towards police control of broadcasting.

On the 31st July, Home Secretary Roy Jenkins in a written reply to a question in the Commons, announced that the commercial radio network was to be limited to nineteen, one fewer than the number of BBC local radio stations. In his announcement to the House, Mr Jenkins explained that the previous administration had envisaged a commercial radio network of up to sixty stations. But the Government had decided to halt development of the network in order that the Annan Committee could make its recommendations. "Nineteen stations," wrote Mr Jenkins, "would be a sufficient number for the Annan Committee to examine."

Thirteen local radio stations had been awarded contracts and six were on the air. They were Capital Radio (London), London Broadcasting, Piccadilly Radio (Manchester), Radio Clyde (Glasgow), BRMB Radio (Birmingham), and Metro Radio (Newcastle). The remaining seven stations which were due to start soon after were Radio Hallam (Sheffield), Radio City (Liverpool), Swansea Sound, Radio Forth (Edinburgh), Sound Broadcasting (Teeside), and Radio Trent (Nottingham).

Six more areas were to be allowed to have commercial radio stations, said Jenkins. They were Bradford, Ipswich, Portsmouth, Wolverhampton, Belfast and Reading. But if problems such as site acquisition offered obstacles to the timings of openings, alternative locations could be considered.

Lord Aylestone welcomed the Government's statement. "Obviously, the authority would have liked to continue with the previously announced plans for 27," he said, "towards the ultimate goal of up to 60. But we are pleased that the Government has agreed to accept the Authority's representations that the new radio system should be continued some way further, rather than cut development off at 13 stations."

Soon after the Authority advertised for further applicants for local radio franchises.

The very last franchise to be announced was the Reading contract. In March 1975 it was offered to Radio Kennet — a company made of many names that had been involved in the first bids for the London contract three years earlier.

The IBA had awarded contracts to nineteen companies. In total, 64 had applied to the Authority since the first contracts were advertised on 4th October 1972. The total population coverage of the full network was 25,570,000. The largest station being Capital Radio with a potential 8½ million listeners in its VHF catchment area. Radio Orwell in Ipswich is the smallest with a potential audience of only 210,000.

What is the future of independent radio in the United Kingdom? The Annan Committee is likely to report its findings either at the end of 1976 or early in the following year. If the Government decide to accept any of the Committee on the Future of Broadcasting's suggestions it will be at least a further two years before any of them are implemented. In the meantime, because of the general political and economic climate of the country, a change of Government will probably occur before then. If the Conservatives are returned to power they will almost certainly authorise the IBA to expand the ILR network to the originally envisaged sixty stations. It is unlikely that they would suspend the Annan Committee again, as they did in 1970, but they will probably not take much notice of its findings.

Annan is expected to report very favourably about independent local radio. Most of the broadcasting industry is agreed that if there are to be any further developments in the field of radio, it should be with local radio. The only arguments are over how it should be financed. The BBC's 20 local radio services are run on incredibly low budgets. The money comes indirectly from the combined radio and television licence fee collected by the Post Office. Attempts to get local authorities to contribute towards the costs of local radio have been made by both the BBC and the Government, but this has been unsuccessful.

The output of independent local radio stations is double, sometimes treble, that of their BBC counterparts which frequently opt in and out of networked services. In all the areas where both a commercial and a BBC local radio station are operating it is the commercial station which is far more popular. One senior executive from ILR once described BBC Local Radio as "part-time broadcasting". "How can a radio station have any identity of its own when it has to keep relaying programmes from Radio One or Two?" he asked "We can interrupt our programmes at any time of day with local news, traffic information or anything that the community needs to know about." The BBC's argument is that its local radio stations can present minority and specialist programmes of a standard and quality much higher than the commercial stations can provide as they can only cater for the interests of the majority.

Annan has been presented with many examples of how commercial radio has been able to provide a service for the community — a service that the BBC would not be able to provide without a considerable drain on its financial resources. Independent Radio is providing a public service without any public expenditure.

But a wealth of technical evidence has also been presented to Annan which indicates that it is possible for the United Kingdom to support a much larger number of low power local radio stations. In view of that the Committee may well propose an increase in both the number of independent and BBC local radio stations.

One of the major factors which is going to influence any decisions, whether by a Labour or a Conservative administration is the success of the existing stations already on the air. Most companies predicted that they would not make a profit until their second or third year of operations. The two London stations, LBC and Capital Radio, between them have lost nearly five million pounds in their first two years of operations. The first station to declare a profit was Piccadilly Radio which had expected to make a loss in its first year. But it will be the smaller stations on which all the attention will be focussed for this is where the IBA and the industry see the future of radio lying. If, for example, Radio Orwell or Plymouth Sound go to the wall it will have serious repercussions for the entire network.

Commercial radio is of course self financing and it must obtain all its revenue from advertising. On average, on each station 40 per cent of the advertising time sold is to local advertisers by the station's own sales team. The remaining sold time is taken up mostly by national advertisers booked through advertising agencies.

Two London companies sell time on a commission basis on behalf of the stations. The two companies, which both emerged from unsuccessful applicant groups for the London franchises, are Broadcast Marketing Services Limited (representing Capital Radio, Metro Radio, Radio Forth, Radio Clyde, Swansea Sound, Pennine Radio, Radio City, and Radio Trent) and AIR Services Limited (representing Piccadilly Radio, BRMB Radio, Plymouth Sound, Radio Victory, Radio Hallam, Radio Orwell, Downtown Radio, LBC, Thames Valley Broadcasting, Radio Tees and Beacon Radio). The managing directors of both groups ran rival sales operations in the sixties during the pirate era. Terry Bate of BMS was the Sales Manager of Radio Caroline, whilst Eddie Blackwell from AIR Services represented Radio London.

The advertising industry is still very sceptical about the effectiveness of radio advertising in spite of the many sales success stories which the stations frequently announce. The Association of Independent Radio Contractors — a body which represents the companies — in a leaflet entitled *Radio Sells!* gives examples like the farmer who bought five 30-second commercials on Piccadilly Radio on a Sunday, inviting the public to go and pick strawberries on his farm — 7,000 people arrived to pick their own strawberries that day! Another example was an electrical discount store in Swansea's High Street which took part in an in-store joint promotion with Swansea Sound. The Police had to be called out to control the crowds and the manager reported "fantastic" trading on the Saturday. He did £9,000 worth of business — so much in fact that he ran out of stock. A further success story from Glasgow is recorded. The popular group Steely Dan were booked to appear at the City's Appollo Theatre and 2,500 tickets had been sold, but at lunchtime on the day they had to call it off due to illness. Only Radio Clyde carried notification of this — but not one fan turned up at the theatre that night.

AIRC also issue monthly revenue figures for all the stations. For the quarter July to September 1975 (when only fourteen stations were operating) £1,875,000 was spent on radio advertising. It is estimated that the gross revenue figure for ILR will top £10,000,000 for 1976. But in times of economic recessions like that to which this country is heading advertising budgets are cut to the lowest levels. In the next few years stations are going to have to keep tight control on expenditure and anticipate falling sales figures.

One of the most important things to any independent radio station is the size of its audience. The advertising industry has insisted on very stringent control and uniformity over the way in which surveys are conducted. Audience research is now carried out under the auspices of the Joint Industry Committee for Radio Audience Research (JICRAR) representing advertisers, advertising agencies and the radio companies themselves. The contract for carrying out the research was awarded to a major independent market research company, Research Surveys of Great Britain Limited (RSGB). Because of the high costs of the surveys most stations only have two a year. The JICRAR specifications are intended to make the research as reliable and accurate as possible for the amount of money that can be spent on it, and also to make the results for each individual area comparable with every other.

The minimum sample size for the larger areas is 1,000 adults and for the smaller areas, 800. Respondents are chosen at random, in accordance with the statistical theory of probability, and are each given a pocket-sized "diary" in which they are asked to record all their radio listening across a week, generally by quarter hours. A compilation of the various RSGB surveys showed that in April 1975, when at that time only ten independent local radio stations were on the air, a total of ten million adults were listening every week to commercial radio. The cumulative weekly audience figure, usually called the "weekly reach", represents all those people who listened to a station at some time during the measured week. The average number of hours for which each of these people listened (typically 10-12 hours per week) suggests that they are "real" listeners, not just people tuning in occasionally and fleetingly. Detailed analysis of results show that there is a very large and growing audience for independent radio. An interpolation of results already received suggests that the total audience to all nineteen ILR station by mid-summer 1976 will reach 21,000,000 (38 per cent of the population of the UK.).

The contract between the Independent Broadcasting Authority and any radio company is on a three-year "rolling" basis — that means that the Authority review the contractors performance at the end of every year. If its performance is satisfactory the IBA will renew the contract for a further three years. If the Authority is not satisfied the contract will not be renewed, but the station will have the opportunity to make amends before the Authority reviews it again at the end of the second year. This effectively gives the stations more security than they would have with a fixed term contract, but also gives the Authority a considerable amount of power over the station. It therefore appears unlikely that any station will ever lose its franchise, as has happened with television programme contractors. The Authority has the power to make changes to a contractor's management, directors, programmes, and even facilities. Although the thought of this amount of control may appear frightening it is only intended to provide a responsible broadcasting service for the public.

A significant development in independent local radio is likely to occur as and when stations pass their break-even points and move into a profit situation.

Plans are already well in hand at several stations for splitting the medium-wave and VHF transmitter outputs during the evenings. It is proposed that more specialist and minority interest programmes are broadcast on the VHF channel while popular music programmes continue on medium wave. Advertising would be carried on both services, but effectively the popular side of the operation would be subsidising the programmes which would attract smaller audiences.

It has taken a very long time for legal land based commercial radio to come to the United Kingdom. It has arrived at a time, which economically and politically speaking has been very depressing. But it is here now, and if it can outlive the financial gloom around it, it will have a very exciting future. In many areas Independent Radio has already proved that it can provide balanced programming that is informative, educational and popular. The final words go to James Gordon, Managing Director of Radio Clyde:

"I think that Independent Local Radio has already shown that it is providing a better public service than the BBC. I resent the implication that those who work in the independent system are not motivated by a desire to serve their communities. Our aim has been clear from the work go — to provide a first class service for the people in our areas which in time will bring its own financial rewards. We are content to be judged on our record, but it would be wrong and unfair if there were to be a prejudice against us simply because we are independent local radio. The message is clear — local radio and independent local radio at that, is here to stay."

APPENDIX A

1) Independent Local Radio

ILR BELFAST:	DOWNTOWN RADIO 293
	Community Radio Services Limited,
	Kiltonga Radio Centre,
	P O Box 293,
	NEWTOWNARDS, County Down,
	NORTHERN IRELAND
	Tel. Newtownards 2491/95 (Offices)
Managing Director:	David Hannon
Chief Engineer:	Hedley Reilly
ILR BIRMINGHAM:	BRMB RADIO
	Birmingham Broadcasting Limited,
	P O Box 555,
	BIRMINGHAM, B6 4BX
	Tel. 021-359 4481/9 (Offices/sales)
	021-359 4011 (Phone-Ins)
Managing Director:	David Pinnell
Programme Controller:	John Russell
Sales Manager:	Reg Davies
Chief Engineer:	Dave Wood
News Editor:	Brian Sheppard
ILR BRADFORD:	PENNINE RADIO
	Bradford Community Radio Limited,
	P O Box 235,
	Pennine House, Forster Square,
	BRADFORD, BD1 5NP
	Tel. 0274 31521 (Offices)
	0274 392211 (Sales)
	0274 392121 (Phone-Ins)
Managing Director:	Stephen Whitehead
Programme Advisor:	Austin Mitchell
Deputy Programme Controller:	Stevie Merrike
Sales Manager:	Mike Waddington

Chief Engineer: John Orson
News Editor: Tony Cartledge

ILR EDINBURGH: RADIO FORTH

Radio Forth Limited,
Forth House, Forth Street,
EDINBURGH, EH1 3LF

Tel. 031-556 9255 (Offices/sales)
031-557 0194 (Phone-Ins)

Managing Director: Christopher Lucas
Programme Controller: Richard Finlay
Sales Manager: Freda Todd
Chief Engineer: Ian Wales
Head of Music: Ian Anderson
Head of Drama: Hamish Wilson
Head of News: Tom Steele

ILR GLASGOW: RADIO CLYDE

Radio Clyde Limited,
Radio House, Blythswood Court,
Anderston Cross Centre,
GLASGOW, G2 7LB

Tel. 041-204 2555 (Offices)
041-221 6615 (Sales)
041-204 0261 (Phone-Ins)

Managing Director: James Gordon
Head of Entertainment: Andy Park
Sales Manager: Peter Elliott
Chief Engineer: John Lunsden
Head of News: Alex Dickson

ILR IPSWICH: RADIO ORWELL

Radio Orwell Limited,
Electric House, Lloyds Avenue,
IPSWICH, IP1 3HV

Tel. 0473 211762 (Offices/sales)

Managing Director: Donald Brooks
Programme Controller: John Wellington
Sales Manager: David Cocks
Chief Engineer: Richard Allison
Head of News: Tim Ewart

ILR LONDON
    ENTERTAINMENT: CAPITAL RADIO
Capital Radio Limited,
P O Box 194,
LONDON, NW3 3DR
Tel. 01-388 1288 (Offices/sales)
     01-388 1255 (Phone-Ins)

Managing Director:	John Witney
Programme Controller:	Michael Bukht
Sales Manager:	Tony Vickers
Chief Engineer:	Gerry O'Reilly
Head of Music:	Aidan Day

ILR LONDON NEWS: LBC 261
London broadcasting Company Limited,
P O Box 261,
Communications House,
Gough Square,
LONDON, EC4P 4LP
Tel. 01-353 1010 (Offices)
     01-353 4671 (Sales)
     01-353 8111 (Phone-Ins)

Managing Director:	Patrick Gallagher
Sales Manager:	Dick Seabright
Chief Engineer:	Mike Barton
Chief Editor LBC/IRN:	Marshall Stewart
Deputy Chief Editor LBC/IRN:	Ron Onions
Output Director:	Peter Robins
Traffic Manager:	Dave Mason

ILR LIVERPOOL: RADIO CITY
Radio City (Sounds of Merseyside)
    Limited,
P O Box 194,
8/10 Stanley Street,
LIVERPOOL, L69 1LD
Tel. 051-227 5100 (Offices/sales)
     051-227 2727 (Phone-Ins)

Managing Director: Terry Smith

Programme Controller: David Maker
Sales Manager: Geoffrey Moffatt
Chief Engineer: Peter Duncan

ILR MANCHESTER: PICCADILLY RADIO
Piccadilly Radio Limited,
Piccadilly,
MANCHESTER, M1 4AW
Tel. 061-236 9912 (Offices/sales)
061-228 6262 (Phone-Ins)

Managing Director: Philip Birch
Programme Controller: Colin Walters
Sales Manager: Richard Bliss
Chief Engineer: Philip Thompson

ILR NOTTINGHAM: RADIO TRENT
Radio Trent Limited,
29-31 Casle Gate,
NOTTINGHAM, NG1 7AT
Tel. 0602 581731 (Offices/sales)
0602 581881 (Phone-Ins)

Managing Director: Dennis Maitland
Programme Controller: Bob Snyder
Sales Manager: Tony Churcher
Chief Engineer: Geoff Woodward
Head of News: John Edwards

ILR PORTSMOUTH: RADIO VICTORY
Radio Victory Limited,
P O Box 257,
PORTSMOUTH, PO1 5RT
Tel. 0705 27799 (Offices/sales)
0705 27755 (Phone-Ins)

Managing Director: Guy Paine
Head of Programmes: Dave Symonds
Sales Manager: Kevin Ward
Chief Engineer: Russell Tollerfield

ILR PLYMOUTH:	PLYMOUTH SOUND
	Plymouth Sound Limited,
	Earl's Acre, Alma Road,
	PLYMOUTH, PL3 4HX
	Tel. 0752 27272 (Offices)
	0752 25744 (Sales)
	0752 27651 (Phone-Ins)
Managing Director:	Robert Hussell
Programme Controller:	David Bassett
Chief Engineer:	Tim Mason
Head of News:	Malcolm Carroll
Head of Women's Programming:	Louise Churchill
ILR READING:	THAMES VALLEY BROADCASTING,
	P.O. Box 210, The Silberts,
	Bath Road, Calcot,
	READING,
	Bucks.
	Tel. 0734 413131
Managing Director/ Programme Controller:	Neil ffrench-Blake
Sales Director:	Michael Moure
Chief Engineer:	Robin D'Earth
Adminstration Manager:	Jean Barclay
ILR SHEFFIELD AND ROTHERHAM:	RADIO HALLAM
	Radio Hallam Limited,
	P O Box 194,
	Hartshead,
	SHEFFIELD, S1 1GP
	Tel. 0742 71188 (Offices)
	0742 78771 (Sales)
	0742 78771/71188 (Phone-Ins)
Managing Director:	Bill MacDonald
Programme Director:	Keith Skues
Sales Promotion Manager:	Darryl Adams
Chief Engineer:	Derrick Connolly

ILR SWANSEA:	SWANSEA SOUND
	Swansea Sound Limited, Victoria Road, Gowerton, SWANSEA, SA4 3AB
	Tel. 0792 893751 (Offices) 0792 894762 (Sales) 0792 893031 (Phone-Ins)
Managing Director:	Charles Braham
Programme Controller:	Colin Mason
Sales Manager:	Gordon Davies
Chief Engineer:	Stan Hordbin
Head of News:	Trevor Curtis
Head of Welsh Programming:	Wyn Thomas
ILR TEESIDE:	RADIO TEES
	Sound Broadcasting (Teeside) Limited, Dovecot Street, STOCKTON-ON-TEES, Cleveland
	Tel. 0642 615111 (Offices) 0642 615333 (Sales) 0642 69257 (Phone-Ins)
Managing Director:	John Bradford
Programme Controller:	Bob Hopton
Sales Manager:	Terry Cassidy
Chief Engineer:	Chas Kennedy
Head of News:	Bill Hamilton
ILR TYNESIDE:	METRO RADIO
	North East Broadcasting Company Limited, Metro Radio, NEWCASTLE-UPON-TYNE, NE99 1BB
	Tel. 0632 884121 (Offices/sales) 0632 884311 (Phone-Ins)
Chief Executive:	Neil Robinson
Programme Controller:	Geoff Coates
Sales Manager:	Tony Hatton
Chief Engineer:	John Russell
Head of News:	Kevin Rowntree

ILR WOLVERHAMPTON: BEACON RADIO
Beacon Broadcasting Limited,
56-57 Queen Street,
WOLVERHAMPTON,
Staffs.
(Temporary Address)
Tel. 0902 22351 ext. 484
(Temporary offices)
0902 29634 (Sales)

Managing Director: Jay Oliver
Programme Controller: Allan MacKenzie

2) Independent Commercial Local Radio

ISLE OF MAN: MANX RADIO
Isle of Man Broadcasting Commission,
Broadcasting House,
Douglas Head,
ISLE OF MAN
Tel. 0624 3277/8/9 (Offices/sales)
0624 4299 (Phone-Ins)

Chief Executive/
   Programme Controller: Peter Kneale
Sales Manager: Sheila McCabe
Chief Engineer: Ewan Leeming
Chief Announcer: Bill Chrisp

3) Other Useful Addresses

BRITISH BROADCASTING CORPORATION,
Broadcasting House,
LONDON, W1A 1AA
(01-580 4468)

INDEPENDENT BROADCASTING AUTHORITY,
70 Brompton Road,
LONDON, SW3 1EY
(01-584 7011)

IBA ENGINEERING INFORMATION SERVICE,
Crawley Court,
WINCHESTER,
Hants, SO21 2QA
(0962 822444)

RADIO LUXEMBOURG,
38 Hertford Street,
LONDON, W1Y 8BA
(01-493 5961)

RADIO TELEFIS EIREANN,
Radio Centre,
Donnybrook,
DUBLIN 4
(0001 69311)

UNITED BISCUITS NETWORK,
Syon Lane, Osterley,
Middlesex
(01-568 8497)

KCN (Factory Radio),
Kimberly Clarke Limited,
Larkfield,
nr. MAIDSTONE,
Kent

RADIO E.M.I.,
1-3 Uxbridge Road,
HAYES,
Middlesex

RADIO BUTLIN,
Entertainments Officer,
Butlin's Holiday Camps,
Bognor Regis,
Sussex. (Enquiries for all camps)

NATIONAL ASSOCIATION OF STUDENT BROADCASTERS,
Vice President (Communications)
Student's Union,
Sussex University,
Falmer House, Falmer,
BRIGHTON,
Sussex.

NATIONAL ASSOCIATION OF HOSPITAL BROADCASTING
  ORGANISATIONS,
255 Greenside,
Euxton,
CHORLEY,
Lancashire.
(Chorley 6029)

NATIONAL ASSOCIATION OF DISC JOCKEYS,
P O Box 23,
HITCHIN,
Herts, SG4 9JT
(0462 50918)

CAMPAIGN FOR INDEPENDENT BROADCASTING,
13 Ashwood House,
LONDON, NW4
(01-203 0861)

FREE RADIO ASSOCIATION,
339 Eastwood Road,
RAYLEIGH,
Essex

LOCAL RADIO ASSOCIATION,
25 Connaught Square,
LONDON, W2 2HL
(01-262 5988)

FREE RADIO CAMPAIGN,
BM — FRC,
LONDON, W1
(01-908 0499)

THE ASSOCIATION OF INDEPENDENT RADIO CONTRACTORS,
20 Tudor Street,
LONDON, EC4Y 0JS
(01-353 5451)

BROADCAST MARKETING SERVICES,
Radio House,
5 Newman Passage, Newman Street,
LONDON, W1P 3PF
(01-580 8682)

AIR SERVICES LIMITED,
Brettenham House (South),
Lancaster Place,
LONDON, WC2 7EN
(01-379 6751)

APPENDIX B
For The Technically Minded.

With the exception of the London MF stations, the basic transmitters operated by the IBA have a power of 1 kW. In the case of 2 kW stations a third transmitter is introduced. This arrangement operates with two of the 1 kW transmitters operating in parallel, while the third is in a standby mode. They are all manufactured by Marconi Communication Systems Ltd. The following is a description of a 1 kW station:

"The transmitter comprises an all solid-state low-power drive unit and a single vacuum tube, a triode output amplifier. The drive unit comprises of a crystal-controlled oscillator operating at four times the operating frequency of the transmitter. The output is fed via buffer and squarer stages to binary dividers. These are followed by a collector-modulator solid-state RF amplifier which provides an output carrier power of 15 W to the grid current of the 1 kW linear output amplifier. The output amplifier uses a single zero-bias air-cooled triode value type 3CX3000F7, which operates with an anode voltage of 4 kV. A pi-network transforms the anode-to-ground impediance to 50 ohms."

In the event of a failure a changeover to the stand-by transmitter is effected in less than three seconds.

One of the features of the IBA network is the use of directional medium-frequency aerials. These arrays comprise up to four mast-radiaters, which are approximately 9o in electrical height, and require site areas of up to 15 acres, which are covered with an extensive buried radial copper-wire earth system.

The Independent Broadcasting Authority publish a Technical Review on Independent Local Radio. It contains detailed features on the engineering planning of ILR, the transmitting stations, the programme input and control equipment, the directional MF aerial arrays and the design and operation of a studio centre. Copies are available to the public, free of charge, from Engineering Information Service, IBA, Crawley Court, WINCHESTER, Hants., S021 2QA.

The following information on ILR wavelengths, frequencies and transmitter information was supplied by the IBA:

A total of sixty ILR stations throughout the United Kingdom was envisaged in the White Paper of March 1971 as the eventual target; and the locations of the first twenty-seven, which would reach about 50 per cent of the population, were later announced by the Minister. By mid-1974 thirteen of these stations were either on the air or the programme companies had been selected by the Authority. In July 1974, however, the Home Secretary announced that only six more stations would be authorised, bringing the total to nineteen, and that further development must depend on the Annan Committee report.

NOTES ON TRANSMITTER TABLES (pages 178-9)

MF Transmitters:
*Until early 1975 London MF transmissions broadcast on temporary frequencies from Lots Road, Chelsea.
†MF omnidirectional aerial.
‡Maximum authorised power.

VHF Transmitters:

NOTES: 1. *Polarization is either Horizontal (H), Circular (C), or Slant (S).*
            2. *ERP is the maximum effective radiated power.*
            3. *Aerial height is expressed in feet above ordnance datum (ft. aod).*

AREA AND COMPANY	MF TRANSMITTERS Site	National Grid Reference	Frequency (kHz)	Wavelength (m)	Transmitter Power (kW)
London News LBC	Saffron Green*	TQ 216 977	1151	261	5.5
London General Capital	Saffron Green*	TQ 216 977	1546	194	27.5
Glasgow Radio Clyde	Dechmont Hill	NS 647 578	1151	261	2
Birmingham BRMB	Langley Mill	SP 160 968	1151	261	0.8
Manchester Piccadilly	Ashton Moss	SJ 925 994	1151	261	0.35
Tyne/Wear Metro Radio	Greenside	NZ 151 627	1151	261	1
Swansea Swansea Sound	Winsh-wen (Jersey Road)	SS 681 966	1169	257	0.8†
Sheffield and Rotherham Radio Hallam	Skew Hill	SK 327 933	1546	194	0.3
Liverpool Radio City	Rainford	SD 464 001	1546	194	1
Edinburgh Radio Forth	Barns Farm	NT 178 842	1546	194	2†
Plymouth Plymouth Sound	Plumer Barracks	SX 490 585	1151	261	0.5†‡
Nottingham Radio Trent	Trowell	SK 506 398	998	301	0.25†
Teeside Radio Tees	Nr. Stockton	NZ 420 218	1169	257	1†‡
Bradford Pennine Radio	Tyersal Lane	SE 197 322	1277	235	0.3‡
Portsmouth Radio Victory	Farlington Marshes	SU 688 052	1169	257	0.8†‡
Ipswich Radio Orwell	Foxhall Heath	TM 212 445	1169	257	0.5†‡
Wolverhampton Beacon Radio	Sedgley	SO 905 939	989	303	0.3†‡
Belfast Downtown Radio	Knockbreckan	J 372 675	1025	292	1‡
Reading Thames Valley Broadcasting	Manor Farm	SU 710 709	1410	210	0.7†‡

VHF TRANSMITTERS

Site	National Grid Reference	Frequency (MHz)	ERP (kW)	Aerial Height ft. aod	Polarization
Croydon	TQ 332 696	97.3	2	905	C
Croydon	TQ332 696	95.8	2	905	C
Black Hill	NS 828 647	95.1	4	1,653	C
Lichfield	SK 164 043	94.8	2	1,400	C
Saddleworth	SD 987 050	97.0	2	1,278	C
Burnhope	NZ 184 474	97.0	5	1,407	C
Kilvey Hill	SS 672 940	95.1	1	752	C
Tapton Hill	SK 324 870	95.2	0.1	950	H
Rotherham	SK 432 913	95.9	0.05	486	C
Allerton Park	SJ 412 866	96.7	5	353	C
Craigkelly	NT 233 872	96.8	1	975	C
Plympton	SX 531 555	96.0	1	513	C
Colwick Wood	SK 597 398	96.2	0.3	436	S
Bilsdale	SE 553 962	95.0	2	2,144	C
Idle	SE 164 374	96.0	0.5	849	C
Fort Widley	SU 657 065	95.0	0.2	420	C
Foxhall Heath	TM 212 445	97.1	1	265	C
Turners Hill	SO 969 887	97.2	1	975	C
Black Mountain	J 278 727	96.0	1	1,748	C
Butts Centre	SU 713 734	97.0	0.25	320	C

Most of the studios of the independent local radio stations are similar in layout. Basically, they consist of a main on-air studio with a second studio known as master control. Both are usually "self-op" — that is operation by the deejays or announcer, and either can be used on air, or as a standby. A number of smaller studios are used for news reading and commercial production.

Radio Hallam has been chosen as a typical studio layout. Studio A is the main studio from which nearly eighteen hours of programmes are broadcast a day. The key to the photograph shows the many pieces of equipment used by the deejays.

As Manx Radio is somewhat different in operation to the IBA and the ILR stations, the technical details are included separately.

Manx Radio commenced broadcasting in June of 1964 from a caravan located on Onchan Head, at that time broadcasting in stereo. The studios were then moved to Loch Promenade in May 1965, and the MF transmitters to a site known as The Eairy in Foxdale, O.S. co-ordinates 779302, and the FM Transmitter to Snaefell Mountain. The studios have moved yet again to an ex Radar Training school on Douglas Head, transmission beginning from this site on the 23rd October, 1969.

STUDIOS:- Manx Radio has two control studios, Master control (M.C.R.) and Production control, with two satellite studios used for interviews, music recordings etc.

MCR. This studio is used as the "live" studio, having priority over all other studios, the Control Desk is a stereo 8 channel 32 input mixer, capable of handling microphones to tape recorders and remote broadcast lines, it is designed for "self-op." The equipment is mostly American, marketed by R.C.A., also it contains a 4 deck endless loop cartridge machine for spot commercials, jingles etc., and Two Rusco 12" Broadcast Turntables with Broadcast Tone arms, the Tape Machines are Series 6 Ferrographs and finally AKG224 Microphones.

PRODUCTION CONTROL. This studio is designed to be compatible with the MCR but it is Mono. Again the desk is an 8 channel input mixer, handling the same inputs as the MCR. The Turntables are Gates 18" Transcription units with Gray research Tone arms.

This studio contains the Master Tape recorder, which is an RCA RT21 Pro. unit which is remotely controlled from the Desk; also the Master Cartridge recorder is in this studio. This again is marketed

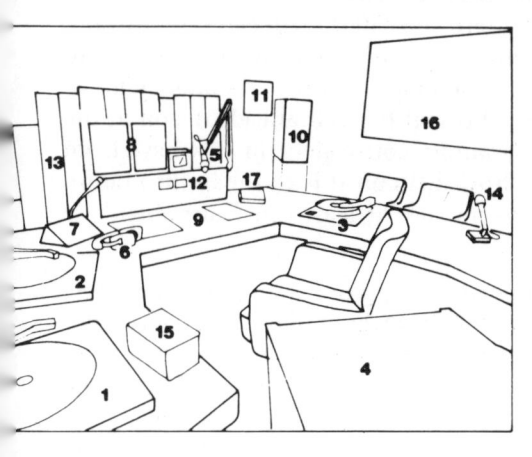

1, 2 & 3   Record Turntables
4   Tape Machine No. 2
5   Presenters Microphone
6   Stereo Headphones
7   Talk-Back Unit
8   Cartridge replay machines
9   Output Controls
10   Rt. Hand monitoring speaker
11   Synchronous Clock
12   Stereo output meters
13   Tape Cartridges
      (Containing jingles etc)
14   Interview Microphone
15   Tape remote control
16   Central Control
17   Cartridge remote control

Studio A at Radio Hallam.

by RCA and is on RT27/BA27 combination. This studio is the control centre for the two satellite studios, and these are used for production of all commercials etc.

TRANSMITTERS:- Manx Radio operates a total of 5 Transmitters, 3 MF (232 main, 232 standby and 188 mtrs.) and 2 FM 89 MHz on Snaefell and 91.2 MHz., all except 232 Main are PYE 1 kW TXes. The Main TX is an RCA 10/5/1kW. Transmitters operated on 1 kW.

APPENDIX C

IF YOU'RE thinking of trying to get a job in independent radio, the first thing you must realise is that you're not the only one. Every day, each station receives dozens of applications for jobs that they don't have available. Another point is that you must realise that independent local radio stations are all small concerns running on tight budgets and limited staff. They don't have the time, the money or the facilities to give anyone training. Normally they are only interested in experienced personnel who know what they are doing.

Most people want to be disc jockeys. There is never a shortage of them. It is estimated that there are 30,000 deejays in Britain, working in clubs and discotheques, or with their own mobile equipment. There are also plenty of unemployed professionals who've had considerable experience who will be well ahead of you in the queue. But luckily most programme controllers on ILR have been deejays themselves and know how difficult it is to break into radio. Therefore they're prepared to include at least one "unknown" in their team.

So, if you are still determined to try your hand, here are a few tips. Firstly, try to get involved in something like a theatrical club. It will give you experience of working on a stage and with a team of people. You'll also learn how to project your voice, and the meaning of words like "emphasis." Secondly, start reading a good daily newspaper. It will help your grammar and keep you better informed about what's going on around you.

You'll only succeed on local radio if you've got the right personality and you're capable of working in a small and very close team.

If you just want an ego-trip, forget it. There's no need for them in commercial radio. Because stations have only a small staff, there is a certain amount of overlap of duties. It helps if you know how to edit a tape and write a script. Hospital radio stations are a very good training ground. They're usually made up of a team of volunteers who give up their spare time to bring a little pleasure to the patients. At nearly every commercial station on the air today, there's at least one deejay who started on hospital radio.

If you don't want to be a deejay, but an engineer, both the BBC and IBA offer training courses. Start with them to gain some experience, then move on to ILR. Alternatively, if you're interested in the advertising side, it is really up to you to go along and sell yourself.

It's very difficult to find a job on the news side of a station. Generally, news staff are only recruited from the local newspapers. As the station is required to broadcast a substantial amount of local news, its news staff must be very well informed about everything happening in the locality.

Most stations advertise vacant posts either over the air or in the local press. You're not likely to get very far by constantly pestering the station's staff. You'll just have to wait until a vacancy is advertised, then be first in with an application.

A disc jockey on BRMB Radio in Birmingham, Adrian Juste, once said that the most important qualification for anyone working in radio, is that . . . "they must be prepared to think, talk and work 'radio,' twenty four hours a day!"

APPENDIX D

The disc jockey is probably the most important person on any pop music station, commercial or BBC. It is his job to link the records, talk to guests, take phone-ins, operate the equipment, log the commercials, read the weather and traffic news and at the same time be informative and entertaining. Not all the independent stations call them disc jockeys. Many refer to them as presenters or on-air personalities. But whatever name is used, if the deejay sounds dull and boring, the listeners will switch off, even when he is playing their favourite records. If a deejay is very good he can command a large audience and a strong following. Most of the nationally known jocks have their own fan clubs.

In September 1975, as independent radio was approaching its second anniversary, the magazine *Radio Guide* held a Dee Jay Poll, in which it invited its readers to vote for their favourite personality. It was in two sections: *Top All-country Deejay*, which could include any deejay who had worked or who was currently working on any local, national or offshore radio station, and *Top Independent Local Radio Deejay*, where readers could only vote for deejays working on their nearest local commercial radio station. These were the results:

THE RADIO GUIDE DEEJAY POLL 1975
Top All-Country Deejay

1.	KENNY EVERETT	(Capital Radio)
2.	NOEL EDMONDS	(Radio One)
3.	TONY ALLAN	(Radio Forth/Radio Caroline)
4.	JOHNNY WALKER	(Radio One)
5.	JOHN PEEL	(Radio One)
6.	ROGER SCOTT	(Capital Radio)
7.	ANDY ARCHER	(Radio Orwell)
8.	ALAN FREEMAN	(Radio One)
9.	ROGER DAY	(Piccadilly Radio)
10.	JOHNNY JASON	(Radio Caroline/Metro Radio)
11.	STEVIE MERRIKE	(Pennine Radio)
12.	TONY BLACKBURN	(Radio One)
13.	JIMMY SAVILLE	(Radio One)
14.	SIMON BARRAT	(Radio Caroline)
15.	DAVE LEE TRAVIS	(Radio One)
16.	PAUL BURNETT	(Radio One)
17.	STEVE ENGLAND	(Piccadilly Radio)
18.	DON ALLEN	(ex-Radio Northsea)
19.	ROSKO	(Radio One)
20.	BRIAN McKENZIE	(ex-Radio Northsea)
21.	CHRIS CAREY (Spangles Muldoon)	(Radio Luxembourg)
22.	ED DOOLAN	(BRMB Radio)
23.	STUART HENRY	(Radio Luxembourg)
24.	KEITH SKUES	(Radio Hallam)
25.	ROBB EDEN	(ex-Radio City)

Top Independent Local Radio Deejay on:

CAPITAL RADIO/LBC
1. Kenny Everett
2. Roger Scott
3. Nicky Horne
4. Dave Cash
5. Tommy Vance
6. Graheme Dene
7. Greg Edwards
   Adrian Love (LBC)
9. Peter Young

10. Kerry Juby

BRMB RADIO BIRMINGHAM
1. Robin Valk
2. Adrian Juste
3. Ed Doolan
4. Brian Savin
   George Ferguson
6. Nicky Steel
7. Dave Jamieson

METRO RADIO TYNESIDE

1. Len Groat
2. James Whale
3. Johnny Jason
4. Dave Gregory
5. Giles Squire
6. Harry Rowell
7. Jeff Brown
8. Big Phil
9. Bill Steel

SWANSEA SOUND

1. Adrian Jay
2. Chris Harper
   Dave Bowen
4. Phil Fothergil
5. Doreen Jenkins
6. Crispian St John
7. Terry Mann

RADIO HALLAM SHEFFIELD

1. Ray Stuart
2. Keith Skues
3. Johnny Moran
4. Mike Lindsay
5. Kelly Temple
6. Colin Slade

RADIO TEES

1. Alastair Perie
2. Brian Anderson
   Leslie Ross
4. Steve Gordon
5. Tricia Ruff

RADIO FORTH

1. Tony Allan
2. Mike Gower
3. Dougie King
4. Ian Anderson
5. Jay Crawford
6. Christopher John
7. Bill Torrance

RADIO CLYDE

1. Dave Marshall
2. Bill Smith
3. Brian Ford
4. Richard Park
5. Steve Jones

RADIO TRENT NOTTINGHAM

1. Jeff Cooper
2. John Peters
3. Peter Quinn
4. Kid Jensen
5. Bob Snyder

RADIO CITY LIVERPOOL

1. Dave Lincoln
2. Fran Scully
3. Paul Easton
4. Robb Eden
5. Norman Thomas
6. Bill Bingham

PLYMOUTH SOUND

1. Ian Calvert
2. Carmella McKenzie
3. David Bassett
4. Colin Bower
5. Louise Churchill

MANX RADIO

1. Ralph Shimmin
2. Alan Jackson
3. Peter Kneale
4. Su Richardson
5. Chris Musk

PICCADILLY RADIO MANCHESTER

1. Roger Day
2. Andy Peebles
3. Steve England
4. Phil Wood
5. Tony Emmerson
6. Peter Reeves

At the time of the Radio Guide Deejay Poll, the following stations were not yet on the air: Pennine Radio, Radio Orwell, Radio Victory, Beacon Radio, Downtown Radio and Radio Kennet (Thames Valley Broadcasting).

Kenny Everett was born on Christmas Day, 1944. His first break in radio came when he joined pirate Radio London. His show with Dave Cash, was one of the most popular on radio in the sixties. He worked for the BBC for a number of stormy years until he was sacked for making comments about the wife of a Transport Minister over the air. Joined Capital Radio when it opened in 1973. *Capital Radio*

Robin Valk's first insight into radio was at York University. He later went to WPHD a radio station in Buffalo, New York state, and stayed there for thirteen months. At the beginning of 1973, Robin was applying for jobs, when he met the management of the consortia applying for the Birmingham franchise. He was earmarked for the job, and when they got the franchise, he got the job! *Roger Barlon*

Len Groat joined Metro Radio after leaving Radio City, a hospital radio station in Swansea and very quickly built up a strong local following. He spends most of his time in the studios working on new jingles. He is also engaged to Swansea Sound presenter, Doreen Jenkins.
R. L. Palmer

Adrian Jay started his career as a guitarist at the age of twelve. Since then he has been a comedian, run a mobile discotheque and worked BBC Radio Bristol. In 1974 when Swansea Sound first went on the air, Adrian Jay became one of the first presenters.

Ray Stuart became a DJ in 1967 when he started working in pubs and clubs in the Sheffield area. Two years later he applied for a freelance job on the local BBC station and was successful. He stayed there learning as much as possible about radio technique, until he moved across to Radio Hallam in October 1974.

Sheffield Telegraph and Star

Alastair Perrie, before joining Radio Tees worked for BBC Radio One and Two where he presented a programme called Gospel Road. He was also host of the BBC 2 television series *See You Sunday*. Since he has been on Radio Tees he has presented the afternoon show *Perrie Pm*.

Tony Allan, born in September 1949 has worked for Radio Scotland, Grampian and Granada Television, Radio Northsea and Radio Caroline. It was through his programmes on Radio Caroline that he built up a very large following resulting in his number three placing in the national section of the poll results. He left the pirate early in 1975, and later joined Radio Forth. *A. G. Ingram*

Dave Marshall first visited Radio Clyde with the intention of selling them some office equipment, but ended up behind the microphone, He was one of the founders of Radio Paisley, a local hospital radio service. He has a wife, a two-year old son and lives in Glasgow. *R. M. Cowan*

Jeff Cooper's radio experience started on the administration side at the BBC. He then became a studio engineer for Radio Veronica in Holland, but returned to England when Piccadilly Radio started. He was a deejay/engineer until he moved to Nottingham for the opening of Radio Trent.

Dave Lincoln joined Radio City when it started in October 1974 and since then has hosted the afternoon 2—6 show. Before joining Radio City he worked full-time for a hospital broadcasting service in Stafford-on-Trent. He is single, in his early twenties and lives in Central Liverpool.

Ian Calvert started his show business career as a disc jockey in local discos and pubs in the Plymouth area. In 1974, he won the Canadian Dry deejay competition and was whisked off to Radio Luxembourg to visit the studios. Ian now presents the only rock show on Plymouth Sound, yet still finds time to run his own mobile discotheque.

Ralph Shimmin, the youngest deejay on Manx Radio presents one of the most popular programmes on the station. He has been working for Manx Radio since 1973, and plays mainly pop music.   *Manx Radio*

Roger Day has been involved in the radio business for a very long time. He is also the holder of the British record for non-stop radio broadcasting. At the beginning of March 1975 he clocked up a seventy-four hour marathon, in which he was allowed only three hours sleep a day, in a special bed set up in the studio. A specially prepared diet was served each day by a Bunny Girl from Manchester's Playboy Club.

Index

A
ACTT, 96, 105
AIR Services Ltd, 81, 116, 164
Aldis, Barry, 23
Allan, Tony, 187
Allen, Liz, 148
all—news station, 62, 63, 84, 87-98, 156-159
American commercial radio, 56
Anderson, Ian, 135, 136
Annan, Lord, 59, 61, 160-163
Archer, Andy, 151
Artists in Radio, 79
Ashton, Norman, 142
Associated Newspapers Ltd, 67, 81, 85
Association of Independent Radio Contractors, 164
Attenborough, Richard, 80. 83, 99, 101
ATV, 80
audience figures, 19, 45, 70, 72, 106, 108, 112, 113, 120, 124, 129, 139, 165
Aylestone, Lord, 73-75, 111-113, 160, 161

B
Bacon, Josephine, 88
Baird, Chris, 144
Ball, Adrian. 84
Ball, Ted, 154
Bance, Greg, 151
Barclay-White, Barclay, 80, 84, 98
Bassett, David, 81, 136-138

Bate, Terry, 81, 120, 164
Bates, Roy, 50, 51
BBC Light Programme, 23
BBC Local Radio, 51, 56, 59, 61-63, 65, 66, 78, 161-163
BBC RADIO ONE, 53-55
BBC RADIO TWO, 53
BBC sponsored programmes, 11
BEACON BROADCASTING LTD, see Beacon Radio
BEACON RADIO, 154, 155
Beaverbrook Broadcasting, 67, 72, 81
Beveridge Committee 1950, 56
Bevin, John, M.P., 46
Bile Beans, 16
Binns, Graham, 80
Birch, Philip, 42, 52, 81, 114-117
BIRMINGHAM BROADCASTING LTD see BRMB Radio
Blackburn, Tony, 53
Blackwell, Eddie, 164
Bliss, Richard, 115
Bollier, Edwin, 60
Bower, Colin, 138
Bradford Community Radio Ltd, see Pennine Radio
Bradford, John, 140, 141
Braham, Charles, 124, 125
Brandon, Tony, 23
Britain Radio, 45, 51
British Broadcasting Company, 10

189

BRITISH BROADCASTING
 CORPORATION, 10, 11, 19, 50, 53,
 160, 161
BRMB RADIO, 84, 111-113
Broadcast Marketing Services ltd, 164
Brown Boveri survey 1967, 61
Brown, Jeff, 118, 119
Brooks, Donald, 150
Bryan, Paul, M.P., 58-60
Bukht, Michael, 100, 101
Burnett, Paul, 23
Burrows, Clive, 132

C
Callan, Paul, 89, 95
Calvert, Dorothy, 48
Calvert, Ian, 138, 188
Calvert, Reginald, 42, 47, 48
Cameron, Douglas, 95
Campaign for Independent Broadcasting, 65
CAPITAL RADIO, 80, 83-85, 98-106, 163
Cartledge, Tony, 148
Cash, Dave, 26, 53, 102, 103
Channel Islands radio plans, 85
Chataway, Christopher, M.P., 60-66, 68, 70-72
City Sounds, 79, 85
Clark, Sir Kenneth, KCB, 73
Clouston, George, 81
Coates, Geoff, 118, 119
Colville, Sir John, 154
Commercial Broadcasting Consultants Ltd. 61-63
commercial radio sites, 68, 72
Community Radio Services Ltd, see Downtown Radio
Conservative Party policy, 57
Cooper, Jeff, 188
Costa, Sam, 22
Crawford, Alan, 39
Crawford Committee 1926, 56
Crozier, Bill, 126
Cudlip, Michael, 89, 94

D
Dale, Robbie, 53
Danvers-Walker, Bob, 24
Darby, John, 133
Davies, Reg, 111
Day, Roger, 116, 189
Dee, Simon, 35
Denning, Chris, 23
directional aerials, 75-77
DOWNTOWN RADIO, 153, 154
Duncan, Peter, 131

E
Eden, Sir John, M.P., 72
Edmonds, Noel, 23
Emmerson, Tony, 117
Emmett, B. P., 131

Everett, Kenny, 26, 103, 186
Everrett, Geoffrey, 23

F
Ferguson, George, 112
ffrench-Blake, Neil, 78, 154, 155
Finlay, Richard, 134
Flint, Michael, 84
Forbes, Bryan, 78, 80, 98, 101
Fordyce, Keith, 23
Francis, Stewart, 147
Free Communications Group, 65
Free Radio Association, 51, 65
Freeman, Alan, 23
Freeman, Roland, 84

G
Gale, George, 95
Gordon, James, 107, 166
Gorst, John, M.P., 61, 64, 68-71
Greater Manchester Independent Radio Ltd, see PICCADILLY RADIO
Green, Hughie, 22, 61-63, 78-79, 83
Griffin, Phil, 117
Grimond, Jo, M.P., 63
Groat, Len, 120, 186
Grundy, Stuart, 23
Guy, Ken, 89

H
Hamilton, Bill, 141
Hannon, David, 151-2
Hargreaves, Alan, 102
Harris, Steven, 145-148
Harrods, 10
Haw-Haw, Lord, 21
Hayes, Keith, 111
Henry, Stuart, 53
Hilversum, 12
Home Office, 161
Horne, Nicky, 102
Hunt, Marsha, 104
Hunter, Sir John, 118
Hussell, Robert, 137, 139
Hutton, Bill, 94, 96

I
INDEPENDENT BROADCASTING AUTHORITY, 61, 62, 65, 67-85, 93, 95-97, 99, 160, 161, 165
Independent Broadcasting Authority Act 1973, 73, 160
INDEPENDENT RADIO NEWS, 63, 87-98, 102, 105, 106, 156-159
Independent Television Authority, see Independent Broadcasting Authority
International Broadcasting Company, 12-21, 81
International Radio Conference, Geneva 1974, 77
Isle of Man Broadcasting Commission, 30-34

J

Jackson, Jack, 23
Jacob, Commander John, 150
Jacobs, David, 22, 99
jamming, 59, 60
Jay, Adrian, 186
Jenkins, Roy, M.P., 161
Jensen, Kid, 144
Jessel, David, 88, 89
JICRAR, 165
Johnson, Duncan, 47, 53
Johnson, Teddy, 22
Jones, Steve, 109
Joyce, William, 21

K

Kelly, Sean, 106
Kelly, Terrence, 142
Kennedy, Chris, 141
Knight, Andrew, 138
Knight, Graham, 144
Knock John Fort, 50
Kolster Brandes Ltd, 12

L

landbased pirate radio, 70, 71
LBC, 9, 21, 83-85, 87-98, 105, 156-159, 163
Levete, Michael, 93-4
Lewis, Bruce, 118
Lewis, Peter, 118
Lincoln, Dave, 188
2LO, 9, 10
Local News of London, Ltd, 84, 99, 102
Local Radio Association, 61, 64, 79
Local Radio Services, 64, 79
LONDON BROADCASTING COMPANY, see LBC
Lotts Road transmitting station, 81, 82

M

MacDonald, Bill, 126, 128-129
MacKenzie, Alan, 94
Maitland, Dennis, 142
Manx Association of Scientists, Artists and Writers, 33
MANX RADIO, 28-34, 180-181
Marconi Company, 9
Marine etc Broadcasting (Offences) Act 1967, 32-34, 49-53
marketing areas, 87
Marshall, Dave, 108, 187
Mason, Tim, 138
Maxwell, Charles, 17
Mebo of Zurich Ltd, 60
Merrike, Stevie, 147
Metropolitan Broadcasting Ltd, see METRO RADIO
METRO RADIO, 118-120
Meyer, Richard, 28-30, 32
Miles, Michael, 22
Mitchell, Austin, 146
Moffat, Roger, 126

Monte Carlo International, see Radio Monte Carlo
Moore, Chris, 38
Moran, Johnny, 23, 126
Morris, Guy, 144
Moss, Don, 23
Murphy, Arthur, 130
Murray, Peter, 22

N

National Union of Journalists, 91-105
Network Broadcasting, 79, 99
Newspaper Society, 58
Newton, Sir Gordon, 94
Nicol, Colin, 23
Nolan, Hugh, 26
North East Broadcasting Company Ltd, see METRO RADIO

O

Oliver, Jay, 152-3
Onions, Ron, 96, 102
O'Rahilly, 37-40, 42, 52, 53
Orchard, Ray, 23

P

Paine, Guy, 150
Paris Broadcasting Station, see Radio Paris
Park, Richard, 109
Parks, Andy, 108-110
Pearl, Geoffrey, 65
Peel, John, 53
PENNINE RADIO, 145-148
Pepper, Tom, 41, 42
Perie, Alastair, 187
Peters, John, 144
PICCADILLY RADIO, 84, 114-117, 163, 164
Pilkington Committee 1961, 56, 57
Pinnell, David, 111
Plugge, Captain L. F., 12
PLYMOUTH SOUND, 136-139, 163
Poste Parisen, see Radio Paris
Prague Plan 1929, 19
Prewitt, David, 65
Prince, Tony, 23
Private Eye Radio Neasden, 72
Project Atlanta, 39, 40, 47, 48
Proudfoot, Wilf, M.P., 51, 52, 70
Pye Ltd, 28, 30

Q

Quinn, Peter, 144

R

Radio Andorra, 25
Radio Atlanta, 40
Radio Brum, 82
Radio Caroline, 32, 35-52, 60, 164
RADIO CITY (Merseyside), 129-133
Radio City (Pirate), 42, 43, 47, 48, 50, 51
"Radio Clothesline", 81, 82
RADIO CLYDE, 84, 106-110, 164, 166
Radio Cote D'Azur, 19

191

Radio England, 45, 49, 51
Radio Essex, 42, 50
RADIO FORTH, 134-136
Radio Geronimo, 25-27
RADIO HALLAM, 126-129
Radio Invicta, 41
Radio Irish Sea, 33
Radio Jackie, 70, 71
RADIO KENNET, see THAMES VALLEY BROADCASTING
Radio King, 42
Radio London, 42, 43, 50-53, 164
RADIO LUXEMBOURG, 12, 14, 16-25, 45, 85
Radio Manchester, 46
Radio Mercur, 35
Radio Mi Amigo, 55
Radio Monte Carlo, 25-27
Radio Nord, 39
Radio Normandy, 12-21
Radio Northsea International, 59, 98
RADIO ORWELL, 151, 152, 163
Radio Paris, 11, 18
Radio Pictorial, 19
Radio Scotland, 43, 53
Radio Sutch, 40
Radio Syd, 36, 44
RADIO TEES, 140, 141
Radio Toulouse, 12
Radio Tower, 44, 45
RADIO TRENT, 141-145
Radio Veronica, 36, 81, 82
RADIO VICTORY, 149-151
Radio 270, 45, 49, 52, 53
Radio 355, 51
Radio 390, 42, 43, 45, 49-51
Rediffusion, 67, 79, 84, 99
Reynolds, Gillian, 130
Richard, Ivor, M.P., 63, 68, 70, 71
Richards, Glen, 150
Robinson, Neil, 119
Rogers, Keith, 151
'rolling contracts', 63, 165
Rosko, Emperor, 53
Rowell, Harry, 120, 151
RSGB, 165
Ruff, Tricia, 141
Russell, John, 111

S
Saville, Jimmy, OBE, 22
Scragg, Julius, 148
Secunda, Tony, 26
Selfridges, 12
Selkirk Communications Ltd, 85, 106
Shenton, Joan, 101
Sherrin, Ned, 78, 79, 99
Shimmin, Ralph, 188
Shivering Sands Fort, 40-42, 47-48
Short, Edward, M.P., 49
Skues, Keith, 47, 53, 126-128
Smedley, Major Oliver, 47, 48
Smith, Terrence, 131

Snyder, Bob, 81, 115, 116, 143-145
Sound Broadcasting Act 1972, 67-72
Sound Broadcasting (Portsmouth) Limited, see RADIO VICTORY
Sound Broadcasting (Teeside) Limited, see RADIO TEES
sponsored programmes, 62, 65, 83
Squire, Giles, 120
Standard Broadcasting Corporation, 106
Steele, Bill, 120
stereo radio, 76
Stewart, Ed, 53
Stewart, Marshall, 95
Stonehouse, John, M.P., 58-61, 63
Street-Porter, Janet, 89-92, 95
Stuart, Ray, 187
Sutch, Screaming Lord, 40-42
SWANSEA SOUND, 122-125, 164
Symonds, Dave, 101, 149

T
THAMES VALLEY BROADCASTING. 148, 162
Thomas, Wyn, 123
Thompson, John, 96
transmitter rentals, 78, 96, 97
Trethowan, Ian, 62
Trinder, Sir Charles, 83, 93
Tynwald (Manx Parliament), 28-34

U
Ullswater Committee 1935, 56

V
Valk, Robin, 186
Vance, Tommy, 23, 26, 101
VHF reception area definition, 87

W
Waddilove, Philip, 65, 79
Wagstaff, Peter, 144
Walker, Johnny, 53
Ward, Sarah, 104
Wardell, Don, 23
Waters, Colin, 115, 116
Wedgwood-Benn, Anthony, M.P., 47-49
White, Geoffrey, 114
White Paper on Broadcasting 1971, 62-66
Whitehead, Philip, M.P., 70, 71
Whitehead, Stephen, 146, 147
Wigmore Broadcasting, 79
Willis, Lord Ted, 78, 79, 99
Wilson, Harold, M.P., 47, 60, 66
WINS, New York, 62
Witney, John, 79, 105
Wood, Phil, 117

Y
Yason, Terry, 26
Yentis, Howard, 88
Young, Brian, 75, 99
Young, Jimmy, 22
Younger, Sir Kenneth, 79

Z
Zam Buk, 16